PRACTICAL THERAPY

WISDOM FOR YOUR RELATIONSHIP, HEALTH, SELF-ESTEEM, AND SPIRITUALITY

DR. ANITA GADHIA-SMITH

Foreword by Former Congressman Jim Ramstad

Practical Therapy
Wisdom for Your Relationship, Health, Self-Esteem, and Spirituality

iUniverse books may be ordered through booksellers or by contacting:

iUniverse
1663 Liberty Drive
Bloomington, IN 47403
www.iuniverse.com
1-800-Authors (1-800-288-4677)

ISBN: 978-1-4620-0422-5 (sc)
ISBN: 978-1-4620-0423-2 (e)
ISBN: 978-1-4620-0424-9 (hc)

Print information available on the last page.

iUniverse rev. date: 03/31/2015

TO MY MOTHER, ANU GADHIA

AND MY FATHER, LALIT H. GADHIA

CONTENTS

FOREWORD

Serving in the U.S. Congress for 18 years, I worked extensively on mental health issues, co-sponsoring the Mental Health and Addiction Treatment Parity Act enacted in 2008. I received input from literally thousands of people suffering from mental disorders and hundreds of professionals trying to help them.

One such outstanding professional is Dr. Anita Gadhia-Smith, a highly respected Washington, D.C. psychotherapist and the author of this book, as well as "From Addiction to Recovery." She is a therapist and author who has a profound impact on the many lives and families she touches.

In her newest book, "Practical Therapy: Wisdom for Your Relationship, Health, Self-Esteem, and Spirituality," Dr. Gadhia-Smith provides a wealth of guidance and wisdom gleaned from decades of work with others.

Every reader of this amazing book will find answers in the seven major components of our lives. With her straightforward, clear and concise writing style, Dr. Gadhia-Smith's book offers simple and practical answers to some of life's most perplexing challenges.

I highly recommend this book for anyone who is struggling or simply wants to change life for the better.

FORMER CONGRESSMAN JIM RAMSTAD

INTRODUCTION

"Practical Therapy" is designed to help you to navigate challenges that you may face in seven areas of your life: relationships, emotional well-being, love, health, self-esteem, prosperity, and spiritual growth. This book was written over the course of twelve years. If you are reading it, you are taking a step to enrich your life. You may choose to read this book from cover to cover, but you can also use it to "snack" on bits of wisdom as you need to. Keep this book by your side, so that you can refer to it when issues come up in your life. It is designed to be simple, practical, and easy to digest.

Wisdom is the ability to discern difference, often between the good and the best. Many of these "therapy bytes" are the result of decades of my own personal growth work, as well as from professional work with patients in my psychotherapy practice. There is no one truth that fits every situation in life; the key is to maintain balance. You will find many paradoxical statements in this book. At one point in life, one concept may apply. Later on, the opposite may apply. It just depends on where you are in your journey. Keep an open mind, use what can help you to move forward, and enjoy!

I wish to express my gratitude to several people who have been my "keys." First, I would like to thank my husband, Dr. Ronald E. Smith. His enduring love, brilliance, wisdom, and support have allowed me to live to my potential in every area of life. I also wish to thank Dr. Inge Guen, "femme extraordinaire," whose presence in my life was the impetus for writing this book, as well as my previous book, "From Addiction to Recovery." Dr. Guen has been a driving force to propel me to take action to pursue my visions and dreams. Finally, I would like to give a very special thank you to Mrs. Melissa Overmyer. Her superior spiritual energies, love, and guidance have transformed and improved the course of my life forever.

Dr. Anita Gadhia-Smith
CONTACT:
WEB: drgadhiasmith.com
EMAIL: drgadhiasmith@aol.com
MAIL: 2500 Q Street, NW, # 237, Washington, DC 20007, USA
TEL: (202) 342-1762

1
RELATIONSHIPS

The most important relationship you will ever have is with yourself.

———•———

In order to have people in your life, allow them to be imperfect.

———•———

Approach your relationships with people from that standpoint of what you can give to them, rather than what you can get from them.

———•———

Even when you dislike or disagree with someone, you can be enriched by your dialogue if you do not judge them.

———•———

Detachment: be brief, be kind, and be gone.

———•———

Other people will not be different just because it is easier for you.

———•———

You can learn how to live from being with people who are dying. The petty little things are just not that important.

———•———

How can you know what the solutions are for other people, when you often do not even know what they are for you?

———•———

No one can make you angry unless you give him permission to do so.

———•———

If you are succeeding in order to get revenge against the naysayers, they still have control over your life.

———•———

Your family of origin may not be your family of choice.

———•———

Maintain humility. Elevating yourself above others leaves you vulnerable to envy, criticism, and loneliness.

———•———

It is not your business what others do with their money.

———•———

Responding to accusations only further draws you into controversy.

If people want to know what you think about their lives, they will ask. If they do not ask, there is no need to tell.

When you resent somebody, it automatically leads you toward feel self-pity.

If people do not reciprocate in relationships with you, back off instead of blaming them.

A fine idea can come from anyone, anywhere.

It is not necessary to defend or answer other people's criticism. Either it will go away, or they will go away if they are unhealthy for you.

It is an unrealistic expectation to expect rational behavior from irrational people.

Instead of trying to fix others, try to gain more understanding of them.

It is useless to expect people to be different than they are. Change your expectations and accept that people are as they are and that you cannot change them.

It is not possible to deal with something that is not yours. Let other people take responsibility for their own issues.

Everybody does not need to know everything.

People only have the power that you give them.

A good way to not respond is to say, "I hadn't considered that."

When someone is not doing what you want, it is not directed against you.

What works for one person may not work for another. Respect this when you are working with other people. Be flexible and open to compromise.

Contrary action is doing something new and different that you are unaccustomed to doing. Even if you do not think differently, you can behave differently.

People come into your life for a reason. They have something to teach you.

You can perpetuate someone's insane behavior by engaging in it. Just because someone throws you a ball does not mean you have to catch it. Just because someone has bad behavior towards you does not mean you have to give it back to them. You can choose to not engage.

Practice letting people have their say without interrupting them.

Weigh and measure your time with difficult people. Boundaries and portion control are keys to sanity. If someone pushes your buttons or is toxic for you, limit your time with them so that you can avoid becoming reactive.

Restrain, reflect, and then respond.

———•———

Codependency is characterized by using your energy to take care of other people at your own expense instead of using it to fill yourself up. Do you want somebody else to get better so that you do not have to?

———•———

Disappearing in your own head is a way of running away and isolating yourself. It is possible to isolate yourself even when you are with other people if you do not make an effort to connect.

———•———

Say it once, and then let it go. Avoid repeating things over and over again. If you keep saying it, you are nagging.

———•———

It is about the way YOU are affected by the relationship, not the way THEY are or who THEY are.

———•———

If you are supposed to repair a past wrong you have done to someone, you will be given an opportunity to do so. You do not have to make it happen. It will just happen.

———•———

Let go of making other people your God and giving them more importance than they deserve.

———•———

You do not need to explain yourself to people. It is okay to say "no" without an explanation or "Thank you, but that doesn't work for me."

———•———

Trying to reason with a toxic person is like trying to blow out a light bulb.

———•———

If people around you are having a disagreement, you do not necessarily have to intervene.

———•———

Anytime the problem is someone else or something else, there is no solution. Keep the focus on your own part.

———•———

Employ a masterful flash of silence. Keep other people's craziness from becoming your own craziness. A well-timed silence can give you control over a situation as an angry reproach never can.

———•———

Let go of trying to figure out crazy people. Just go on and get a life.

———•———

If you want friends, BE a friend. Call people regularly, even if they do not call you. Go out of your way to be there for what is important to them.

———•———

If someone crosses your boundaries, it is not necessary to respond. You do not have to explain why you are ending a conversation.

———•———

Let other people be themselves without trying to change the way they feel.

———•———

Empathize instead of sympathizing.

———•———

With extremely difficult people, agree and then get away. They want to be right, so tell them they are right, and then move on.

———•———

You have the capacity to create the fellowship that you crave.

———•———

If you want to avoid getting involved in other people's stuff, say, "I don't think that's any of my business," or "I don't have any opinion about that."

The best way to get rid of a problem in a relationship is to face it and talk about it honestly.

Set boundaries without building walls and barriers.

If you give advice, avoid the extremes of giving too much or none at all. Pray for discernment and balance about how much to say and when to say it.

Let go of trying to make other people comfortable and just be who you are.

A way to practice not being defensive is to keep your mouth closed.

Opinions are not fact. You can respect another person's right to have a different opinion.

Let go of having a disdainful attitude towards people.

———•———

There are some things it is better not to talk about because they provoke a fight. It is better to keep quiet and protect your peace of mind.

———•———

It is not necessary to have an opinion about other people's opinions.

———•———

Being cheap with money can hurt your relationships and isolate you.

———•———

Offer support without taking on another person's responsibility.

———•———

Honesty involves recognizing what you can and cannot do. It does not always call for full disclosure. You always need to admit your wrongs to yourself and to God, but it is sometimes harmful to another person to reveal everything.

———•———

Plant the seed, do your part, and then move on.

———•———

Refrain from giving unsolicited advice. Unless someone asks for your help, you are intruding.

———•———

Allow different people's opinions to carry different weights.

———•———

Be mindful of your expectations of other people. Sometimes things that are important to you are just not that important to them.

———•———

People do not upset you. You get upset.

———•———

Your biggest objections about others are the things you object to in yourself.

———•———

Assume that everyone has good intent and give them the benefit of the doubt.

———•———

It is not necessary to fall apart in an attempt to get others to rescue you.

———•———

Constant complaining and blaming will poison your relationships.

———•———

Learn to say "no." A way to set a boundary is to kindly say, "That won't work for me." If something is a waste of your time, or even just not the best use of your time, say "no." Sometimes, you have to choose between the good and the best.

———•———

Look at others to observe and learn from them rather than to judge.

———•———

When you start thinking too much about someone, say, "I bless you and I release you."

———•———

Forgiveness does not mean condoning the behavior. It is the willingness to let go of the hurt and leave it in the past.

———•———

Dealing with toxic people is like spiritual jujitsu.

———•———

You never know who is going to be put into your life to help you heal.

Before you decide that someone else is crazy, use the tools you have to keep yourself from being crazy.

If you keep having an expectation of someone and they never meet it, then your expectation is unreasonable. Appreciate what you do get, and then get your other needs met from different people.

You never need to say anything more than twice. If it gets to the third time, people have already heard you say it, and they just do not care.

Your relationship with people will change when you stop being judgmental and critical and start being loving and supportive.

You are not responsible for everything.

People will learn that you have boundaries when you are not always available.

It is okay to tell someone that you do not want to talk about something because it is not good for you.

———•———

If someone is hostile, say "Now is a good time for me to leave." Then just get up and go and do not say anything else. Repeat if necessary.

———•———

It is the person who reacts who starts the war.

———•———

If you are more fully present with yourself when you are alone, you will be more present in your relationships.

———•———

Give other people the dignity of being angry or in a bad mood.

———•———

You have no control over others, but they have no control over you either.

———•———

When you are irritated with someone, try to maintain respect and courtesy for the other person. It is not always necessary for them to know how you feel.

If you have a hard time dealing with a difficult person, deal with them in 15-minute intervals. You can set boundaries around how much of someone you can deal with based on what works for you.

Keep an open mind. Try to listen to other people's perspectives without making assumptions.

Communication and words are not the same thing. Your tone of voice often says more than your words.

It is difficult to communicate with others if you do not know what you really feel. Listen to your own voice.

See the light, not the lampshade. Focus on the qualities that you love about people rather than their shortcomings. This means focusing on what is really important about them instead of their packaging.

Form your own opinions. Sometimes, people who always seem right are simply saying wrong things in a self-assured way.

———•———

Making amends does not mean explaining why you did what you did. It means changing what you are doing today.

———•———

People will respect you more if they know that they cannot fool you.

———•———

Always respect others enough to let them make their own choices.

———•———

Seeing yourself in others is one way to break through your denial about who you really are.

———•———

You do not always need to cut people out of your life; sometimes you can just learn to deal with them differently.

———•———

Extreme oversensitivity can be a form of conceit or vanity, causing you to take things personally. Other people's thoughts and actions do not need to control you. Sometimes, when people are not the way you want them to be, they are not trying to hurt you; their own limitations are being revealed. Most of what other people do is not personal; they are just not thinking about how it affects you. What they do has nothing to do with you. Once you realize this, you can figure out what you need to do to take care of yourself.

In the same way that water finds its own level, relationships find their own level. Just let things happen.

If someone's behavior hurts you, you have a choice about whether or not to feel like a victim.

Although you may not like everyone, you can still treat them with respect.

There is a difference between attachment and connection with people.

Least said, soonest mended.

Treat people as if they like you.

No one of any age can be made to do anything.

———•———

Everyone is entitled to their own feelings.

———•———

When faced with a decision or question, learn to not respond until your inner voice tells you what to do. "Hmmmm" is a complete sentence. When you are not sure how to respond, you can say, "Hmmmm, let me give that some thought."

———•———

Say "no" with a smile.

———•———

Simply look at your part in a situation without trying to teach the other person a lesson.

———•———

Regardless of what you expect, most people will be reasonable.

———•———

Train people to treat you nicely. If they do not, set a boundary with them by not being with them or getting off the phone. Be available only when they treat you well.

———•———

Fighting can be a maladaptive way of trying to connect with a person.

———•———

Avoid being reactive. Just because someone else is mean and nasty does not mean you have to be that way. When agitated, stop and ask yourself what you really want to say. You will never need to apologize for what you did not say. Take the time to get a proper perspective, and then respond when you can be appropriate and constructive. The way that other people behave is not as important as your response. You can save your dignity and have grace by withdrawing from arguments before you get into them.

———•———

Pause. Blurting things out is reactive.

———•———

Maintain a balance between being tolerant of others and holding on to yourself by not giving up too much.

———•———

One way to repair a relationship is to be more present. Another way is to change your attitude towards the person. The rest will follow.

———•———

Recognize that angry people are full of fear.

People change when they are ready.

Other people just do what they do. It is not your fault and it is not because of you. Their behavior does not have to determine how your day is going to go. You can still feel happy and have a good day.

Allow yourself to just be equal to everyone else. It is isolating to feel better than or not as good as others.

When someone irritates you, the best thing you can do is to pause and say nothing. Let them be who they are, then do what you need to do to take care of yourself.

Focus on nurturing relationships that feed your spirit. Do you really like this person, or are you just concerned with getting them to like you?

Rigorous honesty does not always mean saying it out loud.

Learn to disagree agreeably. When someone disagrees with you, let go of being defensive or hostile. Use the same principle when you disagree with someone else.

Over time your thoughts and feelings about others will change.

Acceptance does not require you to like something. It means seeing the true reality and letting go of unrealistic expectations. Focus on the truth about people, instead of what you want the truth to be.

When people irritate you, remind yourself that most people mean well.

Everyone does not have to understand who you are and what you are about. You can be on a different path than someone else.

Work on being the person you think YOU should be, rather than demanding that other people be who you think THEY should be.

In a conflict, try to restrain your communication and handle things calmly. Then look at your own role in the situation. This can lead to things working out in a wonderful way.

As long as you do not react to other people's toxic behavior, they are left standing in it and can have more clarity about their own part. A dramatic response to things really does not change the outcome.

If you are not enjoying someone's company, it is not necessary to be rude. Simply remove yourself.

If you are angry at more than three people in one day, the problem is you.

In trying to help someone, share a little bit of what works for you and then see if the other person wants more. Otherwise back off and leave them alone.

Try to avoid reacting to people in the present based on what has happened to you in the past. For example, your unresolved abandonment issues from your family-of-origin may be resurfacing when you are afraid someone will not show up just because he is late.

You can hold hands with and support another person, but their work is theirs to do.

———•———

The process often matters more than the outcome. In groups, the process is more important than the group product. The important part is that the people come together, give and receive respect from each other, work together, and give everyone a chance to be heard. It is important to tolerate differences and let it be okay that everyone may not agree. Other people's experience is valid, and their points of view matter. This is how to learn to participate with harmony. Participation fosters a sense of belonging with others.

———•———

Let go of trying to change others. Everyone has their own little crazy stuff. People are always going to be acting out in your life. Your peace of mind depends on how you react to it. You can either choose to take offense or not.

———•———

There is no point in trying to be logical with someone who is delusional.

———•———

There are six possible answers to any question: 1. Yes. 2. No. 3. I don't know. 4. I don't care. 5. I don't want to discuss it. 6. I don't want you to discuss it.

———•———

Continually restating yourself is controlling.

People give what they have. They do not have the capacity to give what they do not have, and that does not make them bad people.

It is okay to not like someone even though they like you.

It is not necessary to make someone else's life miserable just because you are having a bad day.

Be still and let the oil and water separate naturally.

Expand your circle of friends constantly so that you do not become isolated. Reach out to new people and bring them into your life.

Have humility. Other people may not be what you want them to be, but you may not be what they want you to be either.

Try to take personal responsibility. Most of what happens to you is self-created.

Focus on WHAT people are saying, rather than WHO they are, or HOW they are saying it.

"What is the right course of action?" is more important than "Who is right?"

Separating, individuating, and becoming your own person can create the space you need to be able to connect better with everyone, including your family.

Instead of trying to have perfect relationships with people, just try to have the best possible relationships with them.

Most people will be indifferent to you. Of those that pay attention to you, most will have positive feelings. Only a few will have negative feelings for you.

If you do not want to react to someone else's negativity, just brush it off.

Setting boundaries means setting limits for yourself. It does not mean making rules for other people.

———•———

Does this person really need this information? You do not need to spell it all out, but you do not need to lie either. Keeping your mouth shut is not necessarily deception.

———•———

People go to others for understanding more than for solutions.

———•———

Avoid trying to reason with someone who is unreasonable.

———•———

Try to behave lovingly. If you cannot do that, just try to show respect.

———•———

If you spot it, you got it.

———•———

The best way to live life is to reach out to another person, not up or down to them.

———•———

Toxic people are just like everybody else, only more so.

What you put into a relationship with someone else will pretty much determine what that relationship is. This also applies to your life in general.

In order to respond to others' excessive requests for help, say, "I cannot help you, but I know where you can get help..."

It takes seven seconds to form an impression of someone.

When your needs are not met as a child, you may unconsciously believe that you are not lovable. This can result in trying to get your needs met through people, places, things, and relationships. These are all forms of faulty dependence.

If you want a social life, take responsibility for your own needs by reaching out to others instead of isolating and sitting around waiting for them to call you.

There is no need to comment on things that do not really matter. Just let them go.

———•———

Detachment is saying: "I can't have this conversation now," or "Let's talk about this later," or "We have different opinions, so let's not talk about this," or "This is too much drama and chaos for me. Please call me when you get things figured out."

———•———

Whether the glass is half empty or half full depends on whether you are drinking or pouring.

———•———

Try to be nice to every person you come in contact with.

———•———

People can put a lot of drama in front of you to avoid intimacy.

———•———

Just because someone says something to you or accuses you of something does not make it true.

———•———

Recognize what is your business and what is not your business. Only involve yourself in things that are your business.

———•———

The most and the least you can do for someone is to pray for them. It is especially important to pray for someone you resent. This will free you from emotional bondage.

———•———

No matter what other people do, try to treat them with courtesy, kindness, and respect. Look for the best in each person and each situation that you encounter. Be grateful for what you DO get from each person in your life, and for the parts of them that you DO love.

———•———

Guilt can make you do more than you need to and take on more responsibility than you should. Recognize when this is happening, and change your behavior. People are willing to dump a lot on you if you are willing to take it on. You have a choice.

———•———

It is not always necessary to offer to help people. If they want your help, they will ask for it. Often, they just want you to listen.

———•———

Avoid criticism of others, but retain good judgment and discernment.

———•———

If something is useful to share with someone, then it is okay to say it.

———•———

Some people need to learn how to stand up, and others need to learn how to sit down.

———•———

Often, when you speak badly about others or gossip, you are projecting your own issues onto them.

———•———

Taking things personally is a form of trying to control.

———•———

If you have a problem in a relationship, just try to clean up your own side of the street. Let the other person figure out his part.

———•———

It is not possible to say "yes," unless you can say "no." If you cannot say "no," you lose your identity, and then people do not know who you really are.

———•———

A lot of relationships are supposed to end after what you were meant to do together is done.

———•———

Setting a boundary involves communication about what you will or will not do. It has nothing to do with the other person.

———•———

Let people vent and have their say instead of reacting and trying to control them. They are not your property.

———•———

Seek your emotional security from spiritual sources. It is inappropriate to demand your emotional security from others. This is a form of taking people hostage.

———•———

On days that you are not fit for human consumption, just try to be graceful. On good days, try to be grateful.

———•———

We see in others what is in ourselves.

———•———

There is a time to choose to not discuss something with another person. You can simply change your attitude and try to be present.

———•———

Give people the dignity of making their own decisions.

———•———

It is not always necessary to answer other people's intrusive questions. You can just smile without saying anything. Sometimes silence is the most powerful response.

———•———

You can be supportive by simply listening and not necessarily give advice. Instead of giving your opinion, you can just state a very general comment, like "That is very interesting," or "Now there is an idea." Sometimes you may not have the solution that someone wants, and you can simply say, "I don't know."

———•———

Dirty dishes in the sink are not personal. They are not a sign of disrespect. They are just dirty dishes.

———•———

If you think the other person is crazy, why are you the only person feeling crazy?

———•———

There are a lot of things that are not worth an argument. Not answering someone or saying, "Yeah, you're right," can usually keep you out of a conflict.

———•———

Refrain from commenting on things you dislike.

People-pleasers are some of the biggest controllers in the world.

If you are picking unavailable people, it might be because you yourself are unable to show up in a relationship. You may be picking people who match your own availability level.

Let people be who they are. It is useless to try to make other people be different just because it is your preference. Accept them exactly as they are.

Sometimes when things look like they are not going well for someone, it may be his chance for grace. Give up thinking you know what is good or bad for anyone, including yourself.

Set yourself up for success. Depend on people who can deliver rather than those who have a history of not delivering.

When a relationship is not going well, both people have a part. Concentrate on your own part, instead of how the other person is irritating you. It is not so important that bad situations magically change as much as that your part be rectified by you.

———•———

It takes a year to build a friendship. It is important to see things over time.

———•———

Pick your battles and discern when you need to speak up and when you need to shut up.

———•———

People need to experience their own struggles in order to have the desire for change and growth.

———•———

What is acceptable for someone else may not be acceptable for you. If it is not acceptable to you, it is unacceptable behavior.

———•———

Neither you nor anyone else in the world is perfect. Let everyone, including yourself, off the hook.

———•———

You can avoid strife in a relationship by being rooted and grounded in love.

In a dysfunctional relationship, 2 + 2 does not equal 4. It never quite adds up.

You know that someone is good for you if you like the way you behave when you are with them.

In order to have mutuality in relationships, teach people how to be there for you, instead of just being there for them.

Each person can only change himself. If you find yourself being drawn into someone's insanity, go around him.

Forgive and forget other people's transgressions. Adopt an attitude of compassion, forgiveness, tolerance, and appreciation.

If the other person is the problem, then there is no solution.

Playing the victim in relationships is a form of controlling.

You can still have relationships with people even if you do not agree with them.

———•———

Even if you only have a five percent responsibility for what went wrong in a relationship, take one hundred percent responsibility for that five percent. No matter how small your part is, own it.

———•———

When having a conflict in a relationship, it is sometimes best to say, "You may be right about that," or "I'd rather not," or "I'm sorry you have that impression." Then stop talking.

———•———

Interdependence is the healthy middle ground between extreme self-reliance and people-pleasing.

———•———

Sometimes the most loving thing you can do is step out of the way and let someone fall.

———•———

When you are uncomfortable or hurt, keep the focus on yourself and speak up about how you feel instead of what the other person did.

———•———

Learn to get along with people whether you have chosen them to be in your life or not.

Give up the need to be right. It is better to be happy than to be right.

Take it easy, keep an open mind, and try to respond rather than react.

If you keep playing "daddy," she will keep playing "little girl."

Keep the focus on your own part of a relationship. Trying to change other people will just give you a headache. Focus on what you need to change and improve about yourself.

Sometimes, the most helpful thing you can do is nothing.

When you disagree with someone, do it with kindness, courtesy and respect.

Treat others with love.

———•———

Having a relationship with someone just because they like you is not enough. You need to like them too. Choose your friends, instead of just letting them fall into your life. There must be mutuality in a relationship.

———•———

An apology is best made when it is not followed by an excuse.

———•———

If someone does not change, that is how it is meant to be.

———•———

Know when to hold them; know when to fold them; know when to walk away; know when to run.

———•———

On communication: "No" is a complete sentence. "Yes" is a complete sentence. It is okay to say nothing at all or to not have an opinion about something. It is also okay to not respond immediately and say, "Let me think about that and get back to you."

———•———

Courtesy and respect for others' needs are an important part of mutual aid.

———•———

When someone disagrees with you, it is not a personal affront. It is just his opinion.

———•———

Honor other people's input even when you feel they are wrong. Tolerate their beliefs, thoughts, and ideas.

———•———

Give up being judgmental, lighten up, and give yourself and others a break.

———•———

Focus on what you have in common with others rather than on the differences. Life is greatly enriched by interaction with other people. There is something good in everyone. Look for the similarities between you and other people, and try to see the light in everyone you encounter. Every person has a gift for you.

———•———

You can have intimacy with others without sharing everything about yourself. People do not need to know everything about you in order for you to be close to them. Nor do you need to know everything about them.

———•———

Go where it is warm. When you need love and support, seek it out from people who can really give it to you. If you seek it out from people who do not have it to give, you may be unconsciously trying to prove to yourself that there is no one there for you. The truth is that love and support ARE available if you seek out what you need from people who can really give to you.

———•———

Compromise in relationships, and at the same time, be true to yourself.

———•———

We are all responsible for our own happiness; we are not responsible for other people's happiness. Trying to take care of other people's feelings is ineffective and exhausting.

———•———

The way to help someone is through gentle guidance rather than by being harsh.

———•———

When dealing with people be firm, factual, and friendly.

———•———

It is not always necessary to respond to what has been said. Sometimes, you can just sit there and listen.

———•———

Determine and ask for what is right for you, regardless of what you think others want or expect from you.

———•——

Your job is to be responsible for your own happiness. It is neither your job nor is it possible to make everybody happy.

———•——

Does this situation really fit you?

———•——

When angry, wait to make decisions until you feel calm.

———•——

Say "no" with gentleness and love rather than with hostility.

———•——

Setting boundaries begins with figuring out what you DO want. It is okay to have elasticity with boundaries and to change your mind.

———•——

Other people have their own paths, destinies, and lives. The most you can do about it is to observe and go along for the ride.

———•——

There is a time for everything: a time to speak up, and a time to be silent.

You are powerless over other people. It is not possible to make them love or respect you. All you can do is be yourself.

Whatever other people do or do not do will not really alleviate your pain.

Perfectionism tells you that you are never good enough. This, in turn, can make you have unreasonable standards for other people.

Expectations are premeditated resentments.

Try to love and accept people for what they are and enjoy them while you have them.

2
EMOTIONAL WELL-BEING

Be grateful for every little thing and enjoy the moment.

If you are wondering if you are crazy, you are not. Truly crazy people never wonder if they are crazy.

Take the time to ask yourself why you are angry. It may be because you are hurt, frustrated, or fearful. Then deal with the real trigger.

To rise above worry, define the situation, face the worst that could happen, resolve to accept the outcome, and work to improve the situation.

If you want to be happy, find something to be enthusiastic about other than comfort and luxury.

Emotional maturity includes: the capacity for concern for others, self-discipline, compassion and involvement with others, self-control, and tempered emotions.

Recoil from all negativity. Take your negative thoughts and try to turn them into positive prayers.

———•———

Take constructive action instead of complaining.

———•———

You will remain stuck in resentment until you look at your own part in the difficulty.

———•———

If you are feeling negative, guilty, or obsessive, bring yourself back to the present moment.

———•———

Do not believe everything you think.

———•———

The bondage of self is the bondage of the mind.

———•———

Sometimes when someone is angry with you they might be trying to push you away. Let them be angry. Try not to react and get provoked into becoming angry yourself. If you do get angry, refrain from saying the first thing that comes into your mind. An angry reaction is almost never the next right thing.

———•———

It is difficult to experience resentment and serenity at the same time.

Fight nothing and nobody.

Most of your pain is created by you, in your own mind.

If you are truly in the present moment, you can deal with whatever is going on.

To detach: change the subject, change what you are doing, and tell yourself to stop.

When you shine a light on fear, there is often nothing there.

Enlightenment means lightening up. Let air come into your life.

Try to keep your mind and body in the same place.

When you are having trouble clearing your mind, and the thoughts keep coming in, stop trying. Just let the thoughts come in one door and go out the other.

———•———

Trying to control the uncontrollable can make you feel crazy.

———•———

It is difficult to go directly from despair to joy. There are steps in between, like sadness, anger, and frustration. Just stay in the process.

———•———

You have a choice about whether you want to think about the bad stuff or the wonderful stuff. Thinking about the wonderful stuff makes it come true.

———•———

If you think you are having fun, you probably are.

———•———

Anger is the birthplace of creativity.

———•———

It is often not important to know why something happened. What matters is how you feel about it and what you want to do about it.

———•———

Try to make a difficult situation better, not worse.

———•———

If you experienced neglect as a child, you may try to turn your workplace into an unconditional loving parent by pushing the limits further and further. If you are doing more and more to test the limits, you are asking, "Will you still love me now...?" The workplace or the government will not love you. They are businesses.

———•———

Resentments are often fueled by shame and self-loathing.

———•———

You can have your feelings, witness them, and not become defined by them.

———•———

Replace worry and fear with prayer.

———•———

There is no reason to be afraid of your feelings. You may be sad or anxious, but that does not mean you will go insane.

———•———

The joyful parts of your reality can overshadow your pain.

———•———

Accept the moment and go through the feelings without projecting ahead.

———•———

Fear is like an old friend. If you accept it, give it a hug, and become friends with it, it will go away.

———•———

It does not always matter whether or not you believe that things will work out. Just keep taking the right steps and actions and ask for help.

———•———

It is not possible to avoid bad times, but it is possible to have serenity during bad times.

———•———

If you are afraid, it is not God talking to you; it is YOU talking to you.

———•———

When you get out of isolation, your problems will shrink.

You can control your thinking, even though you may not be able to control the problems around you.

Try to put a positive spin on everything.

Maintain a balance between freedom and responsibility.

The best revenge is to make your life amazing and fabulous.

It is difficult to really be free from anything until you look at what is on your side of the road.

Resentments are an extra intensity of your reaction to what has happened. Most resentments are irrelevant by the time you get to the end of life. Why hold on to them? Life is short.

Focusing on the negative is a bad mental habit, and it is one that you can break. There are good things to be grateful for everywhere, all the time. Focus on those. Sometimes, it is as simple as being grateful that you have two legs that work, or that you can breathe.

———•———

Believe that good will keep happening.

———•———

Try to enjoy what is in front of you.

———•———

Keep an open mind. Your help can come from anywhere.

———•———

Guard against negative thinking. Keep an open mind, maybe nothing will go wrong. Whatever happens will happen anyway.

———•———

When you are angry, it is a waste of time to focus on the other person. Focus instead on what YOU can do.

———•———

Dealing with anger, fear, and resentment helps you to avoid emotional and spiritual clutter.

———•———

Intense feelings will not swallow you up or kill you. Just accept them, allow them, and ride them out. They will pass.

———•———

You can see beauty when your thoughts are not controlled by fear or resentment.

———•———

Joy comes from obedience to the will of God.

———•———

No matter how you feel, focus on the solution, not the problem.

———•———

Action cures fear. Fear can be dealt with through emotional, behavioral, medical, and spiritual solutions.

———•———

Serenity comes from listening to God and yourself.

———•———

Trust is about letting go of tight-fisted control over life.

———•———

Loneliness and isolation are self-imposed.

———•———

Uncover, discover, and discard.

———•———

When you feel anxiety, remind yourself that God is your constant companion and that He is taking care of you.

———•———

Perfectionism breeds shame.

———•———

You become what you think about most.

———•———

Mental health produces the ability to find the positive in every situation.

———•———

If you want to reprogram your brain, tell yourself, "This is not real. This is just my brain doing this to me."

———•———

As the chaos inside you subsides, the chaos around you will subside.

———•———

Worry will not change the outcome of a situation. Whatever happens, you will have what you need to get through the situation when the time comes.

———•———

A control freak is someone who cannot cope with uncertainty. Setting healthy boundaries reduces the need to be a control freak.

———•———

Resentment does not have a place in the present.

———•———

When you are experiencing anxiety or fear, you may be trying to control the uncontrollable. Turn it over to God and trust.

———•———

If something keeps coming back to your thoughts, you are bothered by it. Once you take action towards resolving it, it will start to fade. When you have done all you can to address it, then it will go away and you will be able to let it go.

———•———

Trying to force things to be different than they are is a source of optional misery.

———•———

Avoid wasting your time being crazy. You do not have enough time or energy to carry around anger, guilt, fear, or shame. Take the unnecessary drama out of your life and put it into living to your potential.

———•———

You have control over whether you are a victim of your own thinking. You can choose your thoughts and take consistent and constructive action to change your cognitive patterns.

———•———

When you feel resentful about something, let go of rehearsing it, nursing it, or cursing it.

———•———

Worrying is meditating on the negative.

———•———

Practice emotional freedom. Allow and express the emotions that you have. The absence of emotions does not make you look perfect.

———•———

Creativity replaces negative thinking with positive action.

———•———

Choose joy in all things.

Growing old is inevitable; growing up is optional.

Serenity is fostered by living in the moment. Worry can be a form of trying to control things that have not yet happened.

Change your thoughts, and change your world.

The greatest tool of the oppressor is the mind of the oppressed.

Acceptance means "drop it." If you are asking "why," you are not in acceptance. Once you are in acceptance, you can move forward into action.

Sanity comes from having a clear plan and then following it.

Try to let go of anger more quickly than you let go of happiness.

———•———

Let other people carry their own anxiety. Avoid letting them use you to do it for them.

———•———

Your life will not stay exactly as it is right now. Change is inevitable. You will be able to use your tools to get through whatever happens.

———•———

While it is good to acknowledge what you feel, you have a choice about where to focus your attention. Focus on the positive and look for the good in every situation.

———•———

Denial is when you do not believe something that is true.

———•———

"Taking offense" means that you have a choice about whether or not you wish to take it.

———•———

It really does not pay to think about something six thousand times. After three times, you have usually done all you can do.

———•———

Accept reality as it is without expecting it to be what you want it to be.

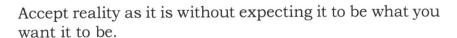

Give voice to your feelings. Fear can have the power to shut you down and cause you to withdraw and isolate if you allow it to. It is no one else's fault that you are afraid. If you do not know how to handle a situation, ask for help from other people and from God.

If you disapprove of what someone else does, avoid commenting on it so that you will not slip into negativity.

Feelings are meant to be expressed, not repressed. They always come out in some way in your life.

Serenity occurs when thinking, feelings, words, and actions are all in sync.

Ask for help. If your mind is not working well, it is difficult to mend it with your own mind.

Drop the pain, take the lesson, and move on.

————◆————

Attitude is everything. Some days everything is perfect and you are miserable. Other days everything is a mess, and you can still have a great day.

————◆————

There are many solutions besides the black and white. Listen to the minority, and to people who disagree with you. You do not know what you do not know.

————◆————

Sometimes walking through a tough time is all you can do.

————◆————

Fear is excitement waiting for an attitude change.

————◆————

Paying what you owe will allow you to live without shame.

————◆————

To turn off the noise in your head, ask yourself, "What am I doing right now at this moment?"

————◆————

You are the author of your own thoughts.

———•———

Feeling fear and grief are part of the growth process.

———•———

To deal with fears list them on paper, give yourself a time limit to feel the fears (10 minutes), and then move on. Your time to be afraid is up.

———•———

Quiet the mind in order to stop feeling crazy and confused.

———•———

If you write a forgiveness and gratitude list every day and say it out loud, you can keep free of resentment.

———•———

Happiness is being calm.

———•———

If you can name it, you can tame it.

———•———

Major life problems may change the quality of your life, but they do not have to ruin the quality of your life.

———•———

When you are not on the path that God has for you, you may feel anxious, depressed, angry, or guilty. These feelings will pass when you take the right actions. You will know they are right because a sense of peace will come to you.

———•———

You need to make peace, not keep the peace. It is not your job to keep peace at any cost by not expressing yourself. This means that sometimes you have to have a fight in order to get to peace.

———•———

If you are resentful, you are in the past. If you are angry, you are in the present. If you are anxious, you are in the future.

———•———

Peace, not excitement, needs to be your first priority. You can have peace and serenity in your life, but you have to invite it in by setting time aside to engage in activities that cultivate it.

———•———

When your mind goes somewhere it should not, start praying.

———•———

"Maybe I'm wrong" indicates open-mindedness.

————•————

You have a choice; instead of going into fear, you can go into trust and know that it is all going to work out.

————•————

Stay focused on the solution instead of the problem.

————•————

Doing something physical that requires your complete concentration will cause fear and anger to dissipate.

————•————

Obsessive thinking is a form of trying to control. When you start obsessing, stop and ask yourself, "What am I trying to control?"

————•————

Just let the feelings come and go instead of trying to control them and allowing yourself to get trapped in them.

————•————

Think in moderation. When you think too much, you can get blocked. You just need to breathe.

————•————

Getting bogged down in the actions of others is the result of an over-developed sense of responsibility. Other people's actions will usually only affect them.

———•———

When it is hysterical, it is historical. An excess of emotion is often triggered by tapping an old, unhealed wound from childhood.

———•———

Behind anger is fear or hurt.

———•———

Peace of mind comes and goes. No one has it all the time.

———•———

If it is too difficult to think positively, just try to think neutrally.

———•———

You are discontented if you complain more than you give thanks.

———•———

Attitude is the difference between being bored and being consistent.

If you are experiencing difficulty, God is either changing you or using you to change somebody else.

You have a choice about whether or not to take offense and become resentful. Choosing not to take offense is an act of the will.

Forgiveness is one of the keys to happiness. Practice forgiveness, and accept what is and move on. This will keep you from getting stuck.

You deserve joy and abundance as a natural state of being.

You have a choice between acceptance and anger. Practice acceptance. Let go of fighting and struggling with the reality of what is. It is what it is.

When you are having a bad day, take a long-term view of your life. Ask yourself if the overall trend has been consistently positive over time. If not, start taking steps to change your direction.

Fear can be the result of self-reliance.

Optimism is the active practice of gratitude.

If you smile when somebody is criticizing you, it will affect you less.

Being judgmental and being a victim are two sides of the same coin.

Choose gratitude. It is not possible to be grateful and angry at the same time.

In order to change negative thinking or painful thoughts, first you need to stop the thinking. You can do this by focusing on what you are doing in the moment. Tell yourself what you are physically doing in the moment, for example, "Right now, I am washing my hands." This will help you to detach from the pain. Then you can shift your focus to something positive.

When you feel resentment towards someone, they are usually unaware of it. They are happy and you are miserable. You can get rid of the resentment by praying for them and wishing them all the good things you want for yourself.

———•———

Confront the old ideas in your mind, and challenge the lies.

———•———

De-cluttering your emotional life means surrounding yourself with people who build you up instead of those who tear you down.

———•———

Leave the past in the past.
Ninety percent of what happens to you has nothing to do with you.

———•———

Sometimes there is no right answer.

———•———

Swearing is a reflection of the unhealed teenager in you.

———•———

If resentment lasts more than four hours, call someone to reason things out.

———:———

Just because the loudest voice is the negative voice does not necessarily make it right.

———:———

Your feelings will be expressed in some way, whether you verbalize them or not.

———:———

To deal with a feeling, name it, claim it, and process it.

———:———

Your level of contentment is equal to your level of compassion.

———:———

Expect the best. "Catastrophizing" or expecting the worst is an improper use of the imagination.

———:———

Getting out of the house, even for a small errand, opens up your mind and gets you out of yourself.

———:———

You live your way to right thinking; you do not think your way to right living.

———•———

What other people think of you is usually not relevant. You cannot control it anyway.

———•———

What you are afraid of is not necessarily what is actually happening.

———•———

When you are in emotional pain, see it as a growing pain.

———•———

No matter how hard things get, you can still count your blessings and be grateful.

———•———

Whatever has been learned can be unlearned. This includes feelings you carry, choices you make, and behaviors you have. Old ways of thinking and behaving can be changed through awareness and by repeatedly taking new actions.

———•———

It is not possible to worry your way to serenity. Worry is a choice that will ultimately impact your state of mind but not the result of the situation. No matter how much you do it, you will not feel peace or be able to change the outcome.

———•———

Courage is the antidote to shame.

———•———

Deal with things as they come up, instead of before they come up. There is no need to anticipate disasters by worrying about what MIGHT happen. Focus on dealing with what IS. If you worry about what COULD happen, you are complicating things unnecessarily and are not in the present moment.

———•———

You do not have to understand everything all the time.

———•———

Acceptance is not approval; it just means accepting things as they are. Acceptance does not mean that you are a doormat. It means that you accept the facts of a situation, and then decide what you want to do about it.

———•———

Feelings are not facts. It is a fact that you feel them, but they may not represent reality.

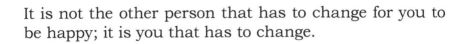

It is not the other person that has to change for you to be happy; it is you that has to change.

No matter what happens, it is exactly the way it is supposed to be. There is no reason to be fearful.
To get a grip, let go.

The answer is in you, not out there. Let go of the idea that happiness is somewhere else. It can only come from within you.

Feelings follow actions.

If you can name it and claim it, then you can do something about it.

Try to limit the time you spend in situations that make you crazy.

Everyone needs sources of emotional refueling. Your body needs food at regular intervals, and your mind and spirit also need regular renewal and refueling. Just like a fussy baby who gets on mama's lap to be soothed, adults need soothing too. People get older and bigger, but they do not really change all that much.

———•———

Part of emotional maturity is the ability to live with unresolved problems and unanswered questions.

———•———

Learn to monitor your thoughts and recognize negative thought patterns. With practice you can interrupt and change them.

———•———

You know you have serenity when you can stand what is going on in your head.

———•———

That was then. This is now. Now what?

———•———

When you feel like a victim, it may be a warning sign that you are participating, either through thoughts or actions, in something that is not in your best interest.

———•———

Choose attitudes and responses that empower you instead of those that leave you feeling like a victim. Choosing to be a victim will keep you from recovering.

———

Guilt is about what you did; shame is about who you are. Guilt is resolved by changing your actions. Shame is healed by repairing how you feel about yourself.

———

Of all the horrible things you have lived through in your life, how many have actually occurred and how many have only occurred in your mind?

———

Let go or be dragged.

———

There are some things that you cannot figure out. It is not always necessary to figure it all out and make the "right" choice.

———

Resolve your guilt. Meet the future head-on instead of head-down.

———

When you resent or blame others, examine yourself to see if you have the same issue.

In order to break obsessive thinking, take action.

It is not necessary to take offense at actions that have nothing to do with you.

When you get wound up or frazzled, slow down and give yourself a chance to find your way. When you are confused, back off and give things a chance to work out. Solutions will come and problems will have a chance to melt away. Even if no one shows up to rescue you, God will step in. He will let you know when the time is right to do the next thing. Let the solutions reveal themselves.

You can be okay even when things are not okay.

Being "emotionally pregnant" means that someone is full of feelings and is feeling them.

Are you dealing with your feelings, or are your feelings dealing with you?

Sometimes, when you do not like someone, it is because you are afraid of them. Even if you do not like them, you still may be able to learn something from them. You can learn kindness from the unkind, patience from the impatient, and tolerance from the intolerant.

———•———

A key to emotional health is gratitude. It is the antidote to self-pity, anger, and resentment. You can cultivate gratitude by praying to want what you have. You do not have to like where you are to find something to be grateful about.

———•———

In order to clean out past emotional issues that you may be unknowingly carrying, ask yourself what makes you angry, hurt, embarrassed, or wanting to lie. If you are always plagued with the feeling that you are doing something wrong, sort it out and recognize what is really wrong and what is really okay. This will help to lift some toxic shame from the past. You will no longer feel like a bad person because you will know where your issues are coming from.

———•———

Learn to let go of the fear of what others think of you, and stop behaving in accordance with what you think their expectations are of you. The perfectionist tries to accommodate everyone and never has an opinion. This can lead to depression and unhappiness. Be who you really are. Being yourself is the ultimate form of self-respect.

———•———

Worrying is an attempt to control or fix things which are beyond your control. Worry is not love, being caring, or being responsible. It is meditating on the negative. Have faith in the positive, not just the negative.

———•———

Accept where you are, what you did, and how you feel. Let go of any anxiety about whether you said or did the right thing. Be okay with the fact that you said or did what you felt at the time, then the grip of it all will let go.

———•———

Become addicted to seeing the positive in every situation.

———•———

Just take it for what it is.

———•———

Examine your fears. What part do you need to take action on? What part is irrational? Many of your fears will never come to pass. Ignoring and not dealing with things you fear only increases the fear. Go ahead and face them.

———•———

When you realize that you are unable to control something, accept it, keep your mouth shut, or walk away. Accept your situation, take right action, let go, and move on.

———•———

Sanity means balanced thinking, not living in extremes.

———•———

Most of the chaos in your life never really happened. It was mostly in your mind.

———•———

Pride believes in entitlement, condemning others, or thinking you are God.

———•———

There is no need to regret the past. If you did not have a past, you would not have learned many valuable lessons, and you would not have the present.

———•———

You do not have to have had the perfect childhood in order to be happy. Your parents had their limitations, but they did the best they could.

———•———

Observe your mind instead of identifying with it.

———•———

How important is this in the larger scheme of things? Most of what is going on around you is not really all that important.

———•———

What price are you willing to pay to prove that you are right?

———•———

Let go of needing to get your own way.

———•———

Most of what you worry about will never happen.

———•———

It is abnormal to act normally in an abnormal situation.

———•———

Boundaries are the primary tool to keep yourself intact when dealing with other people.

———•———

No one can steal your mood unless you give your power over to them.

Do what you need to do in the moment so that you will not have regrets later.

Life happens; joy is optional. Choose your feelings.

Gratitude assessment: what good is happening in your life right now? Take your gratitude vitamin daily. It will keep your life in balance. If you stay grateful and keep a sense of humor, you will always feel okay.

Serenity requires work. Will you go to great lengths to maintain your serenity, or will you just throw it away over any little thing? Try to overlook minor slights and things that are relatively unimportant. Petty trifles can prevent you from enjoying the richness of life. It is not necessary to go mountain-climbing over molehills.

Wait. You do not need to resolve everything immediately.

To process feelings, let them come up, feel them, and then let them go.

What is going on inside is what hurts you, not what is going on outside.

Making amends is like a spiritual antidepressant.

Mantra to yourself: "I am loved; I am safe; it is going to be okay."

Once you are able to admit something, then you can work through it and let it go.

It is okay to have more than one feeling at the same time.

Get more information. Much fear stems from lack of information and ignorance.

When you feel powerless or negative, do something physical.

When you do something good, you feel good. When you do something bad, you feel bad.

Things that happen do not have to be big dramas. They are just incidents, little pieces of life.

When fear hits you, breathe deeply, keep walking, and stay in the present.

Try to keep old ideas from affecting present reality. Separate out the old part, and avoid spinning it into the present.

Most of the time other people do not think that what they are doing is a problem. If you think it is a problem, then you are the one with the problem.

If someone tries to provoke you to anger, try not to defend, react, or argue. Whatever you defend against becomes real.

Do you want justice or peace of mind?

———•———

You cannot change anybody else, so why expend the energy?

———•———

It is normal in life to go through good and bad times. It is fruitless to always try to control things in order to make them be good all the time. Life comes in waves. Try to ride out the tough times with grace and the good times with gratitude.

———•———

It is okay to do what you want to do and just tell people that you are doing what you want to do.

———•———

FEAR is false evidence appearing real.

———•———

Strategies to deal with anger constructively: communicate your feelings, decide not to be a victim, recognize your own part and behavior patterns, refuse to be angry with one person and be taking it out on another, and back off if the other person is angry.

———•———

It is okay to feel crazy when things ARE crazy.

Clean up whatever mess you have created, and leave the past in the past.

Instead of staying in self-pity when things do not work out, take action in other areas and keep moving.

Your opinion about anything really does not matter that much. You do not have to be right. It is better to just be happy.

Shift from thinking about the way you think things should be to working on accepting the way things really are.

Your happiness is your choice.

Not being assertive and speaking up for yourself is a prescription for feeling like a victim.

Positive emotions increase when you focus on gratitude. Spend some time each day thinking about and listing what you are grateful for, both the big and small things.

———•———

Denial of feelings can result in overly-dramatic behavior.

———•———

Are you an optimist or a pessimist? Do you expect the best or the worst in each situation you encounter? You have a choice about whether to focus on the positive or the negative.

———•———

Reality is the truth. It is never totally negative or totally positive. Avoid black and white thinking and stay in the grey.

———•———

Getting too stressed out can make you mean.

———•———

When you are hurting, all you need to do is just get through the next moment.

———•———

Having feelings and acting on feelings are two different things. All of your feelings are okay to have and feel. You can have them without acting on them.

———•———

When you try to get revenge, your revenge usually ends up being on yourself. The opposite of revenge is forgiveness. Forgiveness literally means to untie or loosen; it leaves you free from past pain. It involves letting go of the hope for a better past and lightening up on yourself and others.

———•———

The world in your head is not necessarily the real world.

———•———

To overcome an old behavior, "act as if." If you feel greedy, act generously. If you feel fearful, act boldly. If you feel dishonest, act honestly.

———•———

Try to consciously focus on gratitude each time you have the desire to complain or criticize. This practice will help to transform your thinking from negative to positive and reap huge rewards in every area of your life.

———•———

Concern? Yes. Worry? No. Concern is based in love; worry is based in fear. It is a form of trying to control the future.

———•———

Stay in today. The regular practice of meditation can help train your mind to stay in the present moment. Just focus on what you are doing right now, and try to keep your head and feet in the same place.

———•———

Resentment does not just mean that you dislike something; it is also about obsessing. You feel the negativity over and over again. Resentment is a form of trying to control the past. When you feel resentful, just try to accept things exactly as they are, let go of the past, and stay in the present.

———•———

It is not the mountains but the shoelaces that will trip you up.

———•———

You are usually not upset for the reason you think you are.

———•———

There is no need to figure it all out. Just do what needs to be done in this moment.

———•———

When you do not know what to say or how to handle a situation, just tell the truth.

Wake up every day with the certainty that you do not know what is going to happen that day, and be open to whatever happens. This can help you to let go of anxiety.

Acceptance is not about liking a situation. It is about seeing a situation as it is. If you understand, then things are the way they are. If you do not understand, things are still the way they are.

Although you cannot control your feelings, you can control your behavior. Having fear is not an excuse to act like a nut.

Fear can cause you to unconsciously create what you are defending against.

The unspoken rules of the dysfunctional home are: "don't talk, don't trust, and don't feel." By breaking these rules, you can overcome your childhood wounds and maladaptive behavior patterns.

Always try to take the high ground if you possibly can.

For old wounds: trace it, face it, and erase it.

Being willing to make amends and change your behavior in a positive direction will free you from shame and self-loathing.

When you are overwhelmed, just focus on the small steps you can take.

Worry is like a rocking chair. There is a lot of movement, but you do not really get anywhere.

When you are provoked by someone, delaying your response and being pleasant can help you with ninety percent of your reactive behaviors.

If you stop doing something that is wrong, that vacuum will be filled with things that are right.

You will not die if you tell the truth.

———•———

Fear can have a freezing effect, preventing you from taking action. Usually the thing you fear is much worse than what actually ends up happening.

———•———

If you continue to encounter a similar emotional difficulty, ask yourself," What is familiar about this?" You may be working out an unresolved childhood issue.

———•———

You know that you are making progress when the turnaround time from a bad attitude to a good attitude gets shorter and shorter.

———•———

Just because you do not know what the response to a question will be does not mean that it is going to be negative.

———•———

Thoughts, words, and actions determine feelings.

———•———

Sometimes it is important to learn to get angry. If you did not get angry about things that you should have when you were a child, you might be carrying repressed feelings. This can be hazardous to your physical and mental health. When you start getting angry, it may be a sign that you are growing and healing.

———•———

The degree of your happiness is directly proportional to the degree of your acceptance. Acceptance does not mean that you like what is happening; it just means that you acknowledge that this is what it is.

———•———

Take appropriate responsibility. Blaming others and proving them wrong does not solve the problem.

———•———

The solution to being in a bad mood is to not get into a worse mood. Just wait it out.

———•———

Lighten up and get used to things not being nailed down.

———•———

You never have a bad day, only a bad attitude.

———•———

Just because other people are doing crazy things does not mean that you have to feel crazy.

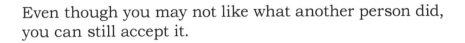

Even though you may not like what another person did, you can still accept it.

It is not necessary to attend every argument you are invited to.

If you can forgive people who have hurt you, you can break old childhood patterns.

If you are angry, walk slowly and breathe deeply.

Contentment is cheerfully accepting the gifts life gives you without raging at life because they are not better.

Although unresolved issues from childhood can improve, some may never leave you completely. Try to refrain from acting out and letting them leak out onto other people and to cause harm to your relationships with them.

Sleep problems and headaches are two signs that you are trying to control too much.

Judgment is a false way of praising yourself.

Having anger is not wrong. Handling it responsibly is what matters. Think before you speak. Learn to step back, sort things out, and then take constructive action.

If you are struggling with a decision, stop and get your head into something else. The answer will often come to you out of nowhere.

Taking responsibility is the antidote to being the victim and blaming others.

Learn how to channel your anger in a healthy, balanced way. It is a powerful energy source. You can use it to tear a house down or to build one. It all depends on the direction that you choose.

Right action leads to right thinking. Right thinking leads to right feeling.

Practice gratitude. Ask yourself daily what is good about your life. Focus on what you DO have, instead of what you think you need in order to be happy. This will keep you away from negative thinking.

———•———

Envy is a hostile form of self-pity.

———•———

When you have a critical or negative voice in your head, ask yourself, "Who is talking right now?" or "Whose voice is this?"

———•———

Clean out your toxic emotions regularly. You can only sweep so many things under the rug until there is no space left between the rug and the ceiling.

———•———

Fear is rooted in selfishness.

———•———

There are many different things to focus on in life. Obsessing is a choice.

———•———

Focusing harder on the problem does not help you fix it; it only digs you in deeper. Focus on the solution, which is usually much simpler than you think it is. Focusing on the positive draws even more positive into your life.

———•———

When you start spinning around a particular topic and are unable to stop talking about it, you are getting into insanity.

———•———

Let go of your shame. Everyone picks their nose.

———•———

Ask yourself what you may be doing to contribute to your own chaos. If you understand what it is, then you can stop it.

———•———

The voice of isolation will tell you that you are different, alone, and that you do not have any friends. This is not true. Accept the good things in your life that are already there.

———•———

Find common ground with others. Focus your attention on what you can share with them, not on what can keep you apart.

———•———

Holding on to blame and resentment hurts you more than anything else.

———•———

Change is easier to handle once you have accepted it.

———•———

Let go of trying to force things that will not work. Just let things happen, instead of trying to force them to fit where they do not fit.

———•———

Focus on enjoying what you DO have and what you CAN do.

———•———

Worry is a self-centered way of trying to control.

———•———

The secret to being miserable is having the leisure time to worry about whether or not you are happy.

———•———

Maintain a balance between being too busy and not busy enough.

———•———

Action is the antidote to worry; inaction breeds worry and obsession.

———•———

Appropriate boundaries result in sanity. If you start to feel anxious around someone, he may be toxic for you. Examine the boundaries that you need to set with them.

———•———

Fearful responses may arise more from habit than from necessity.

———•———

Let go of seeking chaos. This means not picking at things when they are good. Just let them be good.

———•———

Most decisions that you make are not that serious. You can always make another decision. Let go of the fear of making a mistake. You have already made plenty of them. What is one more?

———•———

Sometimes when you are fearful, the tendency is to look for facts to support the fear. Choose to look for facts that support the idea that things will be fine.

———•———

When everything seems to be going wrong, go home and be still. Things will eventually get better.

———•———

There is no shortcut to walking through your feelings.

———•———

Live through your crises as they happen, not before they happen. There is no need to pay the toll until you come to the bridge. Cross the bridge when you get there.

———•———

Faulty thinking is thinking that everything is your fault and that you have to fix it.

———•———

Feelings have a beginning, middle, and end. Hold on and bear them. They will pass.

———•———

You can feel two opposing feelings at the same time. Holding opposites in your head at the same time is one measure of maturity and mental health.

———•———

Partial fulfillment is a reality in all areas of life. Learn to embrace this fact. Come to terms with partial fulfillment in your relationships and other endeavors and accept the fact that you usually cannot have it all just the way you want it.

———•———

Perfectionism is a form of control and striving for the unattainable.

———•———

Live with the fear, and act anyway.

———•———

Fear leads to anxiety, which leads to obsession, which in turn leads to controlling behaviors.

———•———

Try to live in the present moment and stay out of the past and the future. This will allow you to deal with what is actually happening today.

———•———

Strive to be forgiving, understanding, and compassionate. It is toxic for you to stay angry with anyone.

———•———

Losing your peace of mind over a situation is not going to improve it. Stay calm enough to hear the voice of sanity wherever it comes from.

We need regular positive reminders in order to stay happy.

Say prayers of gratitude throughout the day. This will help to change your thinking from negative to positive.

3
LOVE

Love is a decision, not a feeling. It is about how you treat people.

———•———

Take every opportunity to tell or show someone that you love them.

———•———

Praise your partner. Be personal, public, and passionate in your praise.

———•———

Give thanks for the small things that your partner does. If you cannot appreciate the little things, how will you be able to appreciate the big things?

———•———

Let go of inventing things to worry about because you are uncomfortable with happiness.

———•———

While it is important not to act out, it is also important not to repress and internalize anger. This can lead to depression, anxiety, or a later explosion.

———•———

Blame feeds negative emotions. The antidote to blame is taking personal responsibility. Ask for what you want and need.

———•———

Anger can be a powerful source of strength, the rocket fuel needed to make positive changes. It can also transform into gratitude, love and compassion.

———•———

Save the drama for your mama.

———•———

Sulking is unskillful behavior.

———•———

It is not necessary to make your partner pay for your childhood issues. Trying to change others in the present will not correct your past. Trace your anger back to the first time it happened and why it made you angry. Separate that from what is happening now.

———•———

Happiness is not the absence of problems. It is the ability to ride through them peacefully. Instead of striving for illusions and fantasy, focus on what is real.

———•———

Whatever you pay attention to in another person you make real.

———•———

Emotional maturity is about asking for what you want. You need to ask for what you want. If you do not, it is unlikely to happen unless it happens to coincide with another person's plans for himself.

———•———

Learn to recognize the ways you self-sabotage in your relationships, and stop.

———•———

If you are unable to be positive in a stressful situation, just try to be neutral, and avoid going into the negativity.

———•———

Looking at things in a positive light will keep many struggles at bay.

———•———

Do what you need to do in the moment to behave in a loving way so that you will have no regrets later.

———•———

Loneliness reflects an abandonment of self.

———•———

If you are fighting with someone, you can change your mind and stop being upset if you put your mind to something else for a while.

If something is really bothering you, look at your part in it and find out what YOU need to change.

To address fear of loss, remind yourself that nothing and no one that you have are really yours. They belong to God. Be willing to let go of anyone or anything that has to be given back to God, if that is His will.

If you try to hold someone down, you will stay down with him.

If you are in a conflict, take loving action in order to feel better. If you wait until you feel better to take action, you may be waiting a long time. Go ahead and take the first loving action, and then your feelings will change for the better. He who loves first, wins.

Your anger may be telling you that there is unacceptable behavior going on. It is not necessary to tell the other person that it is unacceptable. Remove yourself by physically walking away and let him figure it out for himself by hitting his own wall. If you can stay calm when someone else cannot, he will be more able to clearly see his part, and you will be less likely to have a temper tantrum yourself. There are two times to totally keep your mouth shut: when swimming under water and when angry.

———•———

Forgiving is not forgetting. It is letting go of the hurt. Having unrealistic expectations can set you up for resentment.

———•———

Just because someone throws a ball at you does not mean you have to catch it. You can just let it go by and drop. It is not necessary to respond to everything that happens.

———•———

Pleasure will get you to make promises, but pain will be what really speaks to you to get you to take action.

———•———

Instead of trying harder to love, try differently.

———•———

State your case, and then let go of trying to convince others.

———•———

The right way to do something is whatever feels loving.

If you are feeling uncomfortable in your relationship, it may mean that things are shifting and changing for the better.

———•———

It is okay to not always get what you want exactly when you want it.

———•———

Trust others, but let go of falling for everything people say.

———•———

Sometimes you win by giving up and closing the door on something that is not working.

———•———

Keep your integrity intact. The worst thing is to not get what you want and lose your integrity in the process.

———•———

Do your part and then wait. The more you try to control the outcome of things, the more messed-up they can get. The more you leave things alone, the more they resolve themselves.

———•———

When you blame others, you give up YOUR power to change.

———•———

If you are in the right river, you can go with the flow.

———•———

Birds migrate together because the flying is easier when they support each other. See people as allies, not as enemies.

———•———

There is more than one good or right way to do something.

———•———

Act as if you value your partner if you want your partner to treat you as if you have value.

———•———

Determine what is and is not your responsibility.

———•———

Reserve your judgment. Sometimes something in life seems to be good but then later turns out not to be. Other times, what seems to be bad turns out to be a great gift. What seems catastrophic right now might turn out to be a good thing later.

———•———

Give up your role of being helpless and dependent.

———•———

What you think, you need to say. What you say, you need to do.

———•———

If you give the love that you desire, you will have the love that you desire.

———•———

Sometimes having part of someone is better than nothing at all.

———•———

For everything you lose, you also gain something.

———•———

What are you doing with what you have?

———•———

When you love other people, you love God.

———•———

Keep things simple, and prioritize what is most important.

———•———

Your goals can be about family, relationships, and people, not just about doing and having things.

———+———

You are in entitlement mode if you do not want to contribute.

———+———

The best things in life are not things.

———+———

Focus on what you HAVE, not on what you HAD.

———+———

When you do not know what to do in your relationship, do not do anything.

———+———

Perseverance means not quitting when things get too bad or too good.

———+———

You can have your way more often if you have more than one way. There is more than one way to do everything.

———+———

There is more abundance in the world than you think. There is enough time, money, and love. Your relationships, work, life, and God have more to offer than you may realize.

———•———

Do what you can with what you have where you are.

———•———

Keep an open mind. You might be wrong. Sometimes, being wrong is the best thing that could happen to you.

———•———

Is it going to help you or hurt you to love this person? If it is going to help you, then it is the right kind of loving.

———•———

Take people at their word.

———•———

No one can deprive you of anything in life without your consent.

———•———

In a relationship, positive thoughts have more power than negative ones.

———•———

The "things" that we need most are other people.

———•———

Sometimes, the most loving thing you can do is to stay out of other people's lives.

———•———

People need to work at their relationships.

———•———

Let people take their time and say what they need to say and do what they need to do.

———•———

It is not always necessary to talk so much. It is often unwise to say everything you are thinking and feeling.

———•———

When you are not sure how to respond to a situation, respond with kindness.

———•———

If you want to have good relationships, love yourself first. Then you will have something to give.

———•———

Acceptance is love. Accept people for who they are without expecting them to be different.

———•———

Whether you give to or receive from someone is not the most important thing. The most important thing is the connection between you and the other person.

———•———

Be concerned about others without being consumed.

———•———

You can learn a lot in a relationship by just staying in it.

———•———

Relationships need to find their own level.

———•———

If someone is not a good fit for you, God will see to it that your relationship comes to its natural transition or end. To break up with someone you can say, "I am not sure if it is good for us to spend time together. I will call you when I know."

———•———

Sometimes you need to just allow other people act out and not make a big deal about it. Everyone acts out at times.

———•———

If someone is angry with you, keep throwing unconditional love their way. Instead of reacting to their anger, calmly say, "You didn't have to say that." Then let it go.

———•———

It is more productive to use "I" statements to communicate your own feelings in a challenging communication than "you" statements. For example, "When you do X, I feel Y, and what I would like is Z." If you are using the pronouns "I" and "me," the focus in on yourself and you are setting a boundary. If you are using the pronoun "you," then you are trying to control, which can incite defensiveness and resistance from the other person. Guard against U-turn "I" statements when you start out using "I," but then really end up accusing the other person.

———•———

Sometimes it is best to step aside and let others feel the consequences of their actions. They need to do this in order to grow and change.

———•———

Two people cannot dance unless they are both moving. If you want your relationship to change, change what YOU do.

———•———

Learn to disagree with others with respect. You can be assertive without being adversarial, defensive, or aggressive. Just employ a matter-of-fact attitude.

If you decide you are going to have a good relationship with someone, you will. Cultivate a loving and caring attitude.

You can say whatever you need to say to a person as long as you say it with love.

In relationships, you will get back what you give. Give the other person everything that you want for yourself.

In order to have healthy adult relationships, people need to separate psychologically from their family-of-origin.

Strive for compassion for others. Everyone is trying to swim upstream. The current is stronger for some than for others.

Your partner may not be living up to your expectations, but you may not be living up to his expectations either. Cut both of you some slack, and let yourself and the other person off of the hook.

———•———

Avoid blaming others without looking at your part in things.

———•———

If someone does not respond to your attempts to make contact, then you may need to accept that the relationship is over. A fear of abandonment could cause you to hang on to things too long and too tightly. Just let go. Conserve your energy and see what happens.

———•———

If you disagree with something, you can just say, "Thanks for telling me how you feel."

———•———

No one else is responsible for how you feel. They cannot make you happy or unhappy. Only you can do that for yourself.

———•———

What annoys you about your partner is what is in you.

———•———

If someone is attacking you, avoid responding. If you defend, explain, or engage in responding to accusations, you are behaving as though the other person is right. Just say, "You have a point," or "You might be right." You do not have to respond to what others think of you. If you are unsure what to say, but you do not want to react, just say, "That's interesting."

———

Forgive others by not expecting them to be different than they are and accepting them for exactly who they are.

———

Removing yourself from a situation is not going to change what needs to be changed in you.

———

Before you say something, ask yourself whether it needs to be said, whether it needs to be said now, and whether it needs to be said now by you.

———

If you make a mistake, just admit it and promptly apologize. People will forgive you.

———

Autonomy means caring for someone without losing yourself. You can care for someone without taking care of them in a codependent dynamic.

———

You cannot make anyone of any age do anything.

State your needs once. If the other person does not try to fill them, you may need to get your needs met elsewhere.

Just because someone's feelings are hurt does not mean that you have done something wrong. Even if you have not done anything wrong, try to make things right.

Avoid criticizing and blaming your partner. There is not as much time as you think.

When in a conflict, try not to make it worse. Figure out where the other person is coming from, and try to alleviate his fear.

Forgive the other person before you make your own amends.

No one can give you all the answers. There are some things you have to figure out for yourself.

There is a fine line between help and hindrance.

———•———

You are not the authority on how it works for other people; you barely know how it works for you. Let go of thinking that you know what other people should do.

———•———

Find a balance between what is good for you and what is good for them.

———•———

You have the ability to take care of yourself with anyone in any situation.

———•———

To make a decision about whether or not to be with someone, use the 80/20 rule. If you have eighty percent of what you want in a relationship, that is good enough. Go for it. One hundred percent is very rare.

———•———

Honesty, positive intention, and two-way sharing characterize good communication.

———•———

A harmonious relationship starts with attitude. Be thankful, express appreciation, and aim to make the other person happy. If they are happy, you will be happy.

———•———

Try to be as cordial to your loved ones as you are to others. This means a warm smile, a heartfelt greeting, direct eye contact, focused attention, and words of encouragement.

———•———

Love people and use things instead of using people and loving things.

———•———

When you confront someone you love, focus on the action, not the actor. Gently and constructively focus your feedback on your observations, rather than your conclusions. This may mean commenting less on the "why," and more on the "what" and "how."

———•———

Constructive handling of family problems means remembering that you are on the same side, not making hasty assumptions, being objective, looking for something positive in the situation, and making sure they know you love them.

———•———

Forgiveness does not mean you ignore the wrong action committed. It means that the wrong is not a barrier to the relationship, because you have a new beginning. Keep the offense in perspective; there is more to the other person than their wrong. Try not to humiliate the other person, and try to gain understanding. This reflects unconditional love.

Conflict is inevitable and does not have to hurt your relationship. The absence of problems is not what defines a good relationship; what defines it is how the problems are processed. Conflict can either bring greater isolation or greater intimacy depending on how it is handled.

A true spirit of humility rests upon a non-defensive and loving spirit and a genuine desire to help others.

People can be motivated by many things when they set goals. The most important thing is that their goals are motivated by love.

An intimate relationship only works if you work at it. The three most important things are to be a good listener, speak the truth in love, and always believe the best about your significant other.

You do not need to like everybody, but you do need to love them.

———•———

When a loved one hurts your feelings, say what you feel with respect, and then move on.

———•———

The grace and forgiveness we receive from God must be given to others too.

———•———

Love requires compromise and sacrifice.

———•———

Forgive and love others even when they do not expect it or deserve it. Forgive others over and over again forever. Forgiveness comes not from feelings but is an act of the will.

———•———

It is not enough to just know the laws of love. Live them.

———•———

Money is not love.

———•———

Instead of reacting quickly, pause and ask yourself, "What would God want me to do?"

In order to love another person, the first thing you need to do is take care of yourself. This often means that you are unable to take care of the other person at the same time. When you are not taking care of yourself first, you will become unloving, cranky, irritable, and depleted. When this happens, you are being given a message that you need to get back on track with yourself. Then you will have something to give.

Kindness is one of the most powerful forces in the world. If someone is mean to you, be kind in order to defeat them.

Time over behavior equals trust.

Be around people who want to be around you. It is not necessary for you to do anything to earn their love.

Keep it simple. Focus on your part, come from a place of love, and let it go.

Be gentle with others, but tell them the truth.

———•———

If you are not sure whether or not to say something, put it in the back of your mind and wait. You will not get in trouble for what you did not say.

———•———

People are really trying to do the best they can. It is not your place to judge or criticize them or assess how well they are doing.

———•———

If you want your home life to change, take the lead. It only takes one person changing to alter the dynamics of a relationship.

———•———

It may be difficult to be happy when someone you love is unhappy, but it is not impossible.

———•———

Stick with people who make you laugh.

———•———

Acceptance is agreeing to disagree.

———•———

Make a list of the good qualities about people you love, not the bad ones. This will make them become more lovable.

———•———

Instead of criticizing or complaining, just say, "Whatever..."

———•———

Be constructive or say nothing.

———•———

Be the person you want to attract.

———•———

What you admire in others reflects the admirable qualities that you possess or desire.

———•———

Your attitude towards others comes back to you.

———•———

Find a way to say what you mean without being mean.

———•———

Concentrate on your common bonds with others rather than your differences.

———•———

Being dissatisfied with the other person is really just a manifestation of dissatisfaction with yourself.

———•———

The longest journey you ever take is from your head to your heart.

———•———

You can choose not to take offense when people treat you badly. Just start over.

———•———

Put unity first. Give up that desperate urge to prevail.

———•———

If you stop analyzing others, you will have a lot more free time and serenity.

———•———

When you are having difficulty with someone, you are probably both afraid and anxious. Many people go directly to anger when they are afraid. It is better to just hug the person and say, "We'll figure this out."

———•———

Learn to accept both the good and the bad in the people you love.

Women fall in love with men when they are together; men fall in love with women when they are apart.

It is often better to gently suggest ideas than to give advice.

Conflicts happen because you have chosen to either pick a fight or engage in one.

Sometimes if you ignore bad behavior, it is more likely to disappear.

Whatever you do to others you do to yourself even more.

Rely on humility before intelligence.

An important part of communicating is listening. Try to really listen to your partner. Active listening involves restatement, clarifying, and summarizing.

Although perfect communication may be difficult, remove as much misunderstanding as possible.

Ask for what you want. The other person cannot read your mind any more than you can read his.

It is important to express your love to others in the ways that they want, not just in the ways that you want to give it to them.

Be kind; everyone you meet is fighting some sort of battle.

Everyone has their own way of working things out.

Let people throw a fit when they need to. You are not obligated to get wrapped up in it.

Listen objectively without interrupting, and be non-judgmental.

———•———

Intimacy comes from opening up, sharing more, and trusting God, not from restricting what you share.

———•———

Acting out of love is something to be done for your own serenity.

———•———

You can be a loving person without giving up yourself, your beliefs, your values, and your desires.

———•———

Sometimes love means doing and saying nothing.

———•———

Just because you do not love someone's behavior does not mean that you cannot love them.

———•———

Keep your hands off of your partner's life, and focus on managing your own life.

———•———

Look for the ways that people are showing their love for you.

———•———

Take responsibility for your own happiness rather than hinging your happiness on another person. You are not an extension of someone else.

———•———

If your boundaries are crossed, think not about what the other person needs to change but rather about what YOU need to change.

———•———

Let go, and let other people do the things they are going to do without feeling responsible for them.

———•———

Fight or flight mode does not allow you to maintain unity, respect, or integrity with another person. Speaking up and speaking out does allow you to maintain those things and learn positive conflict resolution.

———•———

It is not important to figure everything out. Just try to be loving.

———•———

Respect the limits of other people. Avoid expecting people to fill you up or fix you and then criticizing them for falling short.

———•———

Accept the people you love as they are, without trying to change them.

———•———

The best gift you can give others is your positive energy.

———•———

Let go of trying to connect with people when they are crazy. Leave them alone.

———•———

Intimate relationships are like mirrors. What you see in the other person is what is reflected back to you about yourself to inform you and to help you to grow spiritually.

———•———

When you are really baffled by someone's behavior, try to understand where they are coming from.

———•———

Being in a relationship does not require you to give yourself away and then resent the other person for it.

———•———

Try to keep a proper perspective about what is worth fighting about and what is not. Let go of things that are not important enough to fight about.

———•———

To avoid getting into an argument and to practice responding with compassion, say "You might be right about that" or "I see your point of view."

———•———

You will attract people who are at your level of development and emotional health. As you invest in improving yourself, you will attract healthier people.

———•———

Not having a life can lead to having an affair.

———•———

Autonomy means holding onto yourself and keeping your own identity. At the same time, you can also be part of a couple, family, or group. Act autonomously, but also keep a focus on maintaining unity.

———•———

Be assertive, but do no harm. Find the balance between keeping the peace at any price and insisting too much.

———•———

Feeling sorry for people is not love.

———•———

Whatever you appreciate, appreciates.

———•———

Give love without giving yourself away.

———•———

Forget about selfish things, and be interested in people.

———•———

Say, "Bless them, change me."

———•———

When someone is behaving badly, they are probably going through a difficulty. Send them good energy instead of adding more negative energy to the situation.

———•———

Just because you are involved with someone does not mean that you are responsible for making it work. Some things are not meant to work.

———•———

It is better to have loved and lost than to live with a psycho for the rest of your life.

Practice good behavior, and then do no more.

The quality of who you are is more important than what you know.

God's will is a loving agenda.

Let others have their own emotional experience. Say, "I know you're angry right now. I'm going to have to go because I can't share this with you."

If you keep getting angry with someone, change your expectations so that they are realistic.

Gratitude is like a Swiss army knife; it is useful in many situations.

Keep the toxic people out of your life, and let the love in.

———•———

If you have to spend time with someone who is difficult, try to compliment him repeatedly. This keeps your focus positive.

———•———

Let your judgment give way to compassion, empathy, and love. Other people are just living their own lives and you are living yours. You have not had their experiences.

———•———

Two people can be in conflict, even though no one is wrong.

———•———

Hold firm and clear boundaries with others with an attitude of gratitude and love.

———•———

Be independent, not codependent.

———•———

Opening yourself up to giving opens you up to receiving.

———•———

Intimacy is sharing. You have to know yourself intimately before you can have intimacy with someone else.

When you give someone a gift, are you giving it for them or for you?

Fill your own needs yourself rather than expecting your partner to fill them.

If someone needs to be upset with you, let them do so. It is not appropriate to deprive others of their own experiences.

It is more loving to be firm, honest, and direct than to be wishy-washy.

Detachment does not have to separate you from people. It can bring you closer to them because you can take care of yourself and feel safe. It means creating healthy boundaries or keeping a distance from something, not cutting it off completely. The love remains intact.

Are you looking in the mirror or the microscope?

Strive to cultivate generosity of spirit.

———•———

Adopting another person's habits can be a way of trying to connect. It is not necessary to become the other person in order to connect. Maintain your own values and identity.

———•———

Keep your heart open, and allow yourself to get close to other people.

———•———

You have to endure what you do not forgive.

———•———

You will attract more people when you keep yourself peaceful and serene.

———•———

Make decisions from a place of love rather than from fear or reactivity.

———•———

Do not give up just because things are not perfect.

———•———

Sometimes, a partner will act up because he misses you, is trying to connect, and does not know how to say, "I want you."

———•———

Make the best of what you have.

———•———

You are powerless over those who may be hurting you. The only power you have is to not react. It is not necessary to react just because you have been provoked.

———•———

Stop, reflect, and adjust. Calm the disturbance before it happens.

———•———

Gratitude is the antidote to complaining. Ask yourself if what you are about to say is going to contaminate or contribute to the situation. Experiment with refraining from complaining or criticizing for ninety days, and you will most likely experience a positive transformation in yourself and your relationship.

———•———

Grief is an act of love. It is not necessary to be afraid of it or to control it.

———•———

You have to go through the pain to get to the healing.

———•———

Try to be as courteous to the people you love as you are to others.

———•———

There is nothing you have to do to earn someone's love or kindness.

———•———

Freedom is not meant to be used for self-indulgence. It is meant to be used to love one another.

———•———

Giving up the expectation that others will never abandon you is a sign of maturity. You are not capable of never abandoning them, so you should not expect them to give you something that you cannot give. Abandonment is not always bad. People need time for themselves in order to do what they are meant to do. It is not personal. Accept them for who they are and what they offer you without fault-finding, criticizing, or having perfectionistic expectations of them and yourself.

———•———

The "one that got away" was supposed to.

———•———

Try to look at people the way God looks at them. See them through the eyes of God.

———•———

There does not always have to be a right and a wrong.

———•———

Underneath any situation with anyone there is always love.

———•———

Try to see situations from the other person's point of view.

———•———

Your response to love is even more important than the love being there because you have to give up self-reliance to let the good in. Just show up and let the love inside.

———•———

If you are giving love from the right place in your heart, it will be for fun, without expectation, and for free. If you are not giving in this way, examine your motives.

———•———

In order to love someone, you are not required to approve of what they do. You just need to accept them as they are. Other people do not always want or need your opinions. Sometimes, you can just keep it simple and not say anything, or you can just say, "You might be right," and leave it at that.

———•———

Minding your own business allows others to be themselves.

———•———

What do you need to let go of before you can be loved?

———•———

If you love someone, leave them alone. People like who they are. They are not necessarily interested in changing to become who you want them to be.

———•———

The most important things to remember in life are that we love each other and that we all have the same heart.

———•———

Do not base your opinion of your relationship on one bad day.

———•———

Working with others is more effective when you come from a place of love rather than from a place of control.

———•———

You can have intimacy with someone without agreeing with them.

———•———

Do not put the people you love most on the back burner.

———•———

Kindness is the mightiest force of all.

———•———

Go where the love is, not where you want it to be.

———•———

You can start a relationship in trauma but end it in love.

———•———

Speak with love and act with kindness.

———•———

If someone is mean to you, love them anyway. It is not about your relationship with them. It is about your relationship with God.

———•———

You only need one person to believe in you to change your life.

———•———

The practice of love is a spiritual discipline.

———•———

Love and focus on the best in people, and let go of the rest. Let them be what they are.

———•———

You can love and forgive people even though they did not do what you wanted them to do in your life.

———•———

How can you spread love today?

———•———

The heart prevails over the mind.

———•———

We are all attracted to what we are.

———•———

Love does not walk away, people do.

———•———

The opposite of love is not hate, it is indifference.

The minimum of love is respect.

If you want to be loved, love.

Loving is a higher function than thinking. Love is stronger than intellect.

If you focus on taking loving action, the situation will eventually remedy itself.

Let go of demanding that other people behave in a way that you think is appropriate.

Trying to determine other people's motives is a form of trying to control. You will feel less stress if you just assume that other people have a good motive.

Having healthy boundaries means that you are doing what YOU want to do rather than overindulging the other person.

Acceptance allows you to stop fighting.

Be honest with yourself and others about what you really want.

Let go of trying to control. Let the good things that are supposed to happen, happen. Let the bad things that are supposed to happen, happen.

When you are reactive to your partner, you are willingly making the choice to give your power away.

Dyslexic behavior is when you pay attention to people when they do something negative, but ignore them when they do something positive.

Say the truth. Just try to communicate what is going on with you to the people you love, no matter what is going on with them. Communication is a skill. Say something, and let the other person process it. Then see how it unfolds.

———•———

Love transforms people.

———•———

The basis of any intimate relationship is friendship.

———•———

Going through trauma and difficulty can show you how much love there is in the world.

———•———

People often seek out relationships with others who have what they are lacking.

———•———

A conflict will occur in every relationship. Either the two people will deal with it and get closer, or they will walk away.

———•———

If you give someone something, give it with no strings attached.

———•———

Learn to love people unconditionally, no matter what they have done to hurt you. It is not your responsibility to fix them, but you do still need to love them. If you try to fix them, their pain will transfer to you. Let them fix themselves, and just try to love them.

Spread out your dependency needs. One person or one relationship cannot give you everything.

Regarding your partner, the most important things are that you are together and that you are alive.

The journey of life is about learning to love yourself and others. Try to behave in a loving way to everyone you encounter.

Take the initiative to have your own life, make your own friends, and be your own person whether you are in a relationship or not.

Learn how to love the person that is in front of you instead of the person you want to be in front of you.

Approval is not love. It is not necessary to turn people into authority figures. When you confuse approval and love, you may seek approval from people who represent an earlier figure in your life, in order to get the love you always wanted. People-pleasing is so exhausting that you may end up leaving the relationship just to be able to relax and be yourself.

———•———

Love comes through forgiveness. The basis for forgiveness is our common humanity. Forgiveness is not forgetting, it is letting go of the pain. Allow yourself and others to be imperfect.

———•———

Act with love for others AND in your own best interest.

———•———

The world is better when men are men and women are women.

———•———

It is enough to have a percentage of someone you care about. It is not necessary to have one hundred percent of everyone.

———•———

Keep doing the next loving thing one minute at a time.

———•———

People will still love you no matter what.

———•———

Life is short. Time is short. Avoid taking people you love for granted. Try to make sure that your side of the street is clean before people die.

———•———

Just because people die does not mean that the relationship is over or that you cannot continue to heal that relationship.

———•———

There is something lovable about everyone. Everyone deserves love and respect.

———•———

Nothing can come of intelligence or imagination without the involvement of love.

———•———

You will often send a stronger message of love through your behavior and actions than through your words.

———•———

In order to give love to someone, you must have it for yourself. It is also difficult to receive it if you cannot give it.

———•———

People need to be heard, even if the problem has already been solved.

———•———

In order to allow people their dignity, let go of doing for them what they can do for themselves.

———•———

Love and sex are two different things; each enhances the other.

———•———

Learn to be able to disagree and still love.

———•———

Whenever you have a choice, take the path of love, and things will work out.

———•———

One of the best things you can ever say to anyone is "It is going to be okay."

———•———

The most loving thing you can ever do for your children is to improve yourself.

———•———

It is almost never a mistake to tell the truth to a child.

———•———

Seek love from people who have it to give. It is not possible to win the love of someone who has none to give.

———•———

Listen for love in other people's words and actions. Try to discern what they are really trying to say.

———•———

In a healthy relationship both people maintain their own identities, AND they do things as a couple.

———•———

Try to maintain unity in your family. What is good for the group is good for you.

———•———

Christmas is about touching base with people you love.

———•———

There is enough love to go around.

———•———

Let go of your resentments, and love your loved ones unconditionally before you lose them or before they become ill.

———•———

Try to nurture the people you love in a positive way.

———•———

There are many right choices and possibilities for love. Let go of the belief that there is only one right person for you.

———•———

Fear of abandonment is not in reality abandonment. If you struggle with a fear of abandonment when your relationship is going well, cultivate more faith. Work on not abandoning yourself when you get into a relationship. This means continuing to take care of yourself, standing up for yourself, and expressing yourself honestly about what you think, need, and feel. If you find yourself trying to control another person, you have abandoned yourself. Just because you may have been abandoned either emotionally or physically as a child does not mean that it will keep happening to you. You have some control over what happens now.

———•———

Ground rules in a relationship with someone you love: 1. No abuse; 2. No threats to leave; 3. No active addiction; 4. No cheating.

———•———

Love and worry do not necessarily have to go together.

———•———

If you cannot love others unconditionally, try to love them with fewer conditions.

———•———

There are four types of love: philia (brotherly love, affection); eros (erotic love); storge (familial love); and agape (unconditional love). Philia is love between friends. Eros is the honeymoon love that you feel at the beginning of a romantic relationship, before you have seen the other person's faults and still believe they can do no wrong. Storge is the innate love that you feel for family members. Agape, or mature love, is the highest form of love and is an act of will. It often costs you something or involves sacrifice. Agape is cultivated when you behave in a loving way no matter how you feel, or when you have seen people's faults and then choose to love them anyway.

———•———

Learn to love the life you are in.

———•———

If you are bothered by old behavior, yet are still practicing the behavior, it is not old behavior. It is current behavior. To overcome it, "act as if." This means that if you feel angry, act as though you have compassion. If you feel impatient, act as if you have patience. You can get your negative character traits under control by acting the opposite way that you feel when they come up.

———•———

Everyone deserves love, even those who have treated you badly.

———•———

The essence of all healing is love.

———•———

What can you do each day to bring more love into the world?

———•———

Inconsistent love can be addictive, like gambling. It can keep you going back for more. Perfectionism can be born from unpredictable and intermittent reinforcement of love. You believe that if you are perfect enough, you will get the love that you want.

———•———

Resentments keep you from being able to love and be loved.

———•———

Children need to know that you will love them no matter what.

———•———

We are all equally important.

How you feel is not as important as how you behave.

An open mind is an open heart.

Marriage forces you to overcome selfishness. If you choose to leave for the wrong reasons, you may be choosing to go back to selfishness.

Listening is an act of love.

Unity is achieved through communication.

There is no need to use a cannon when a fly-swatter will do.

Let your attitudes and actions reflect love.

Being yourself with authenticity allows you to truly exchange love with others.

———•———

You can only give what you possess. It is difficult to love others if it is not within you.

———•———

Focus more on what is right than what is wrong.

———•———

Learn to hold on to yourself, even when you love someone.

———•———

Love is the trump card. Always do the loving thing when you do not know what to do.

———•———

Time is short. Live your life. Love in your life. Give in your life.

———•———

4
HEALTH

Physical self-care clears your thinking. Emotional well-being changes your thinking. Spiritual growth directs your thinking.

———•———

You form your habits, and then your habits form you.

———•———

Let go of the small things that bother you. If you have the big ticket items, like health, stay grateful.

———•———

Take responsible actions on a daily basis to maintain your own health and well-being.

———•———

Repressed anger can be an underlying cause of anxiety.

———•———

If you keep doing the right thing, a shift happens. It is like taking an aspirin and the headache goes away, although you do not quite know when it happened.

———•———

Keep what is important and what is not in a proper perspective. Few things are worth losing your peace of mind.

Go as fast as you can without rushing or hurrying, and you will continuously be at rest.

Every day, try to slightly change an old pattern of behavior that limits you.

More is accomplished through steady perseverance than by force.

Sometimes it is not necessary to solve a problem right away in order to feel better.

Try to restrain yourself from doing what you know has not worked in the past.

You are capable of doing much more than you think you can. Tell yourself that you can do it. Then ask for guidance.

If you have not been watering your flowers, it does not make any sense to dump a truckload of water on them. It is more effective to water them a little bit every day.

———•———

Right living means being committed to your values and being consistent about what you do to take care of your health.

———•———

It usually requires more time to get ready to do something than to actually do it.

———•———

When problems come up, there is no need to panic. Just figure out how to solve them.

———•———

Base your physical goals and visions on sound spiritual and emotional values.

———•———

If you are unable to make a decision, start moving in one direction and see how it feels. If it seems like a lot of things are getting in your way, re-evaluate.

———•———

Just for today, take a tiny risk in inching forward. Keep reaching, without getting ahead of yourself.

———•———

Deepening insight results from thoroughness.

———•———

Just start from where you are and keep going. It is not necessary to reconstruct the past unless it will help you move forward.

———•———

Ask God, and allow yourself to receive strength and endurance.

———•———

Strive to put more ease into your life. Overusing time is a form of self-debting, and can leave you feeling anxious, stressed, and pressured.

———•———

Eat the elephant one bite at a time. Instead of jumping to the big step, start small. If you want to change a big thing, start with one small change. There is no need to worry about things ahead of time. Just plan, and then take things a step at a time.

———•———

Weigh and measure your time very carefully. Too much down time can be isolating. Too little down time can be depleting.

———•———

Rid yourself of anger and resentment; they keep you depleted and less able to work towards your goals.

———•———

Do the little things you can do to make your life easier. Guard against taking on more than you can actually do and then ending up exhausted and unable to go for the best.

———•———

Know your limits and respect them so that you do not compromise your well-being.

———•———

The more you focus on taking care of yourself, the better job you do in all of your affairs. You do not need to live your life running on empty.

———•———

Sometimes you can only see how far you have come when you see what you are not doing anymore.

———•———

A good goal for each and every day is to enjoy yourself.

———•———

Do what needs to be done to maintain good health. Willingness does not necessarily include liking or wanting to do something.

———•———

What choices are you overlooking in your life?

———•———

Have a self-care routine each day, but be willing to modify it as your needs change.

———•———

Trust your feelings. When something does not feel right, it probably is not right for you.

———•———

A habit can be changed. Just take it off and put on another one. If you do something for twenty-one days, it becomes a new habit.

———•———

Let your actions be intentional. Stop and think before you do something.

———•———

The fear of doing something is usually worse than actually doing it.

———•———

Live fully; live big. Focus on the actions right in front of you. The time to live is NOW, not when you get to some point in the future.

———•———

Instead of trying to do it, do it.

———•———

Strive for excellence, not perfection.

———•———

Separate your well-being from your bank balance.

———•———

Do you want to stand at the banquet table of life eating a Snicker's bar?

———•———

Do one thing each day towards your goal.

———•———

If you can make time for worry or resentment, you can make time to get help.

———•———

Putting your health and well-being last is a form of self-sabotage.

———•———

Maturity means taking responsibility for yourself.

———•———

Allow yourself to receive the help that is offered to you.

———•———

Go ahead and face it. Avoidance can prolong the pain and is no safer than exposing the truth.

———•———

If making a change is frightening, the fear will lessen if you make an effort every day.

———•———

Seek help in places where you can really get it.

———•———

Consistency is the key to a breakthrough. Taking things a day at a time gives your life momentum. Develop consistent practices and focus on incremental improvement. What do you need to do today to improve your health?

———•———

Pay attention to the little things. Big things start out in small ways.

———•———

Anger can be a response to stress and taking on too much.

———•———

The more you practice a healthy behavior, the easier it becomes.

———•———

Just because something can be done does not mean it has to be done.

———•———

You may be powerless over people, places, and things, but you are not helpless. Take constructive action for your well-being.

———•———

If you are not sure if you should take a self-caring action, just go towards it, and make the decision when you get there. Instead of asking other people what to do, ask yourself. Make a decision based on what feels right to you instead of because somebody else wants you to.

———•———

Invest time, money, and energy to maintain your health.

Action gives you traction.

The smallest hole can sink a ship.

There is no one right way to do anything.

Do the worst first.

Take the time to get information before you act.

Where you end up is not determined by chance. It is the result of a series of choices that you have made over a long period of time.

Regardless of what it costs you in money, evaluate whether it is worth the emotional cost.

If one thing moves, everything moves.

———•———

When something is really big, just take the next right action and have faith that things will unfold as they should.

———•———

Solve one issue at a time. You can just make day-to-day decisions that are small and trust that God is going to help you.

———•———

You need to build time for self-care needs in to your daily schedule. This is not goofing off.

———•———

Always put your self-care ahead of your business needs.

———•———

A full life is characterized by balance. Maintain balance between work, fun, family, and spiritual activities.

———•———

Put your energy into things that enrich your life.

———•———

Sometimes, the right action is to do nothing.

———•———

Be as careful about time and self-care as you are about money. For example, when it is time to eat or sleep, do that. Be disciplined about the fact that your well-being comes first.

———•———

Take time for things that impact your health.

———•———

Over-commitment leads to living on fumes and is a disservice to yourself and others.

———•———

Establish the prudent middle ground between fear and recklessness.

———•———

What really nourishes you?

———•———

Instead of complaining, try to solve your problem.

———•———

Just because you do something once does not mean it is over.

———•———

Stop compulsively giving away your time, energy, and money because you do not feel that you deserve to use your resources to take care of yourself.

———•———

Trust your own intuition and perceptions, regardless of what others say.

———•———

What is good for you is good for everybody around you.

———•———

Spend as much time with others as is good for you.

———•———

Rather than trying to think your way into feeling better, act your way into it.

———•———

Treat yourself well and try to put ease into your life. Let go of being stern and militant with yourself.

———•———

Your needs are legitimate. Stop dismissing them as childish.

Just because you are good at something does not mean you have to take it on.

Take time out for yourself in order to tend to yourself and not get too enmeshed with other people.

Keep things simple. Do what you can do when you can do it. You do not have to do everything, all the time.

Give to others without taking from yourself.

Find ways to be gentle with yourself instead of being hard on yourself. Give up doing things that do not need to be done.

Beware of energy vampires who leave you feeling drained. Drop them. Cut out time with people who bring you down.

Focus more on what you need than on what other people want.

———•———

Express your wants and desires so that you will not feel depleted.

———•———

If you keep banging your head against a brick wall, it is not the wall that will break first.

———•———

Caring about someone else does not require you to neglect yourself.

———•———

It is not necessary to do it perfectly every time. It is good enough to just try to do better.

———•———

It is appropriate for you to attend to your own needs. It is inappropriate for you to attend to everyone else's needs, ignore your own, and then end up feeling resentful.

———•———

You never know where your help will come from. Keep your mind and options open.

———•———

Sometimes, taking care of yourself means not thinking about what is bothering you.

———•———

Lighten up, take better care of yourself, and have more fun.

———•———

When you start to trip, bump into things, or fall, slow down. You are doing too much.

———•———

If you are not sure whether something is in your best interest, ask yourself, "Is this well with my soul?"

———•———

It is not about what is happening to you. It is about what you can do.

———•———

If you are feeling fearful, first determine whether the fear is real or imagined. Then discern whether there is an action you can take today to alleviate the fear. If not, let it go.

———•———

Acceptance does not mean that you have to like it. It just means that you have to do it because your well-being depends on it.

———•———

Try to be realistic about what you expect of yourself. When you are feeling impatient or unreasonable, you have taken on more than you can handle. Over-extending yourself is a form of dishonesty, either with yourself or others.

———•———

Take no actions unless you know they contribute to your well-being or to the well-being of someone else.

———•———

Tell the truth about what you feel.

———•———

A breakdown can lead to a breakthrough.

———•———

Confidence comes from slowing down.

———•———

Move a muscle, change a thought.

———•———

If it is difficult to deal with something, put it down and deal with something else. Focus on what you CAN do.

———•———

Most days include times when you feel okay and times when you do not.

———•———

Well-being is found in pursuing things that are attainable. Focus on the choices that are available to you.

———•———

Instead of putting energy into worry, put energy into constructive action. Action is the remedy for worry and obsession.

———•———

To restore yourself: meditate, pray, read, talk to someone, take a break, exercise, eat, and socialize.

———•———

Try to not lose your temper. Period. Keeping yourself calm is easier than recovering from an emotional hangover.

———•———

When you start feeling crazy, stop activity, be still, and focus on the next thing you need to do to take care of yourself. If you do not talk to anyone and just sit and isolate, you will spiral down. In order to cultivate support, you must ask for it.

———•———

Do a few things every day just because you enjoy them.

———•———

Abusing yourself emotionally or physically will make you feel unclean.

———•———

Getting better does not always mean feeling better.

———•———

Sometimes the ordinary, little activities of life are exactly the next right thing to do instead of some spectacular wrong thing.

———•———

Maintain balance. Taking time off for renewal and restoration is not a luxury, it is essential.

———•———

Well-being comes through the help of a good advisor, putting in your best effort, focusing on your purpose, and using all available resources to help you.

———•———

The three principles for being good to your body are: 1. Keep it free from toxins or anything that contaminates your body or spirit; 2. Care for your body through rest, exercise, and nutrition; 3. Control your body through discipline and by training it to do what you want it to do.

———•———

True self-indulgence is not about eating or drinking whatever you want; it is about taking care of yourself.

———•———

If you are not one hundred percent, avoid stressing yourself out even more.

———•———

You gain energy by expending energy.

———•———

If you lose your peace, you lose your joy. If you lose your joy, you lose your strength.

———•———

If you are spiritually fit, you can always be busy and never feel stressed.

———•———

Living in freedom begins with self-discipline.

———•———

No matter what is going on in your life, you still need to enjoy what you can and have fun. Make time in your schedule for fun, relaxation, and creativity.

———•———

If you want to hurry up, you need to slow down.

———•———

If you are thinking of ingesting something you should not, ask yourself, "Do I love myself or do I love the...."

———•———

It is not worth the risk of getting off your self-care plan to please other people.

———•———

Keep it light; there is no need to carry around extra physical weight or extra mental weight.

———•———

It is more expensive to overwork than to underwork.

———•———

Maintaining a healthy plan or eating is not just about the food. It is about spiritual fitness and discipline.

———•———

Comprehensive self-care means attending to your physical, emotional, and spiritual well-being.

———•———

Part of self-care is de-cluttering and upgrading the small things in your life.

———•———

Love the busy life, not the frantic life.

———•———

It is not about what you are eating. It is about what is eating you.

———•———

When you stop taking care of yourself, you lose your voice.

———•———

If God can rest for one day of the week without the world falling apart, it is probably okay if YOU rest.

———•———

It is not necessary to put stress, pressure, hurriedness, and worry on yourself in order to motivate yourself. Choose a new way of being.

———•———

Focus on what you are doing in the moment. When you are washing dishes, wash dishes.

———•———

Writing out your worries is a good way to turn them over to God.

———•———

It is difficult to do anything for anyone else if you are not taking care of yourself first.

———•———

Hitting a crisis will often make people realize that they need to make important changes.

———•———

When you realize that change needs to happen, it usually does not happen right away. It happens inch by inch.

———•———

You can change before you hit rock bottom.

———•———

By asking for what you want and attending to your needs and self-care, you will not allow yourself to become invisible.

———•———

The more structure you have, the more freedom you will have. For example, plans for spending, food, exercise, and work allow you maximum freedom to live fully.

———•———

Writing and journaling will help you to own your own reality.

Moving your body helps you move through your feelings.

The modern day form of violence is rushing.

Everyone needs recalibration every day.

What lengths will you go to in order to take care of yourself?

The answer is not putting something IN your body or ON your body to fill the hole inside of you.

Get your rest, get your sleep, and try to think positively.

Clutter in the environment leads to clutter in the mind.

Being exhausted and overworking are ways of avoiding your well-being and your life.

———•———

Buy yourself some space between impulse and action.

———•———

Put your health first.

———•———

You do not have to live in extremes by either depriving yourself or indulging yourself too much. You can be reasonable, have guidelines, and find the balance.

———•———

Meditation reveals to you who you are. Let go of looking for who you are in people, places, and things. Who you are is already in there.

———•———

It is not necessary to depend on something outside of yourself to change your mood. It will change on its own.

———•———

Sometimes compulsive shopping is rooted in loneliness.

———•———

There are two times when you will slip from your self-care: when you are being too hard on yourself and when you are not giving yourself any treats.

———•———

Try to be rigorous, not perfect.

———•———

The more you take care of yourself and the more balance you have in your life, the more things will roll off your back.

———•———

Trust your own rhythms for each day.

———•———

When you do not have physical strength, ask God for spiritual strength.

———•———

What will make you feel better is not what goes into your body; it is what comes out of you into the world.

———•———

Practicing a self-care program with discipline frees you of the disease of "more."

———•———

In order to gauge what is really going on, you need to be quiet. Be still, trust, and wait for the right direction.

———•———

Attending to your self-care allows you to give back.

———•———

When you say "no" to something that is not good for you, you say "yes" to something better.

———•———

The problems do not cause the addiction. The addiction causes the problems.

———•———

Abstinence is about keeping what is harmful to you out of your body. Living in freedom begins with abstinence from toxic substances and results in joy and clarity of thought.

———•———

Slower is faster and more permanent.

———•———

Food is not for celebration. It is medicine that your body needs, like fuel.

———•———

Acting on a compulsion does not make it go away, it makes it grow.

———•———

Physical problems do not have to undermine your spiritual connection.

———•———

Taking healthy actions will lift your spirits and self-esteem.

———•———

Stress is a resistance to what is. Let go of fighting reality.

———•———

You may not be feeling well, but you may still be doing well.

———•———

Sometimes taking care of yourself means doing something, and sometimes it means taking a break.

———•———

Heart disease and neuromuscular disorders can be manifestations of anger lodged inside of you.

———•———

Work daily to keep your stress level down. If stress is not managed, it can give you physical diseases that may kill you.

———•———

Meditation: when the water is still, you can see all the way down to the bottom. When the waves are moving, you cannot see anything underneath. Meditation allows you to see so much more. It is as though your eyes have been opened.

———•———

What is good for your health is good for the health of people around you.

———•———

Instead of going, going, going because you feel anxious and running yourself into the ground, sit still, feel the feelings, and ask God to remove them. It works.

———•———

When you relax and concentrate, you can do what you need to in the time you have.

———•———

One of your purposes is to take care of the gifts that God has given you, especially your health and your body.

———•———

Be mindful of your expenditures of time, money, energy, and emotions.

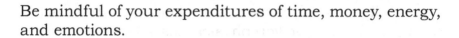

If you fail to plan, you plan to fail.

Let life move at God's pace. Nothing you do is going to make it move any faster anyway.

Choose what you put into your body based on the nutrition it gives you. Adopting a healthy food plan does not mean that you have to like it, just that you have to do it. Stay on it. It is easier to stay on it than it is to get off and try to get back on it.

You will have less physical illness if you do not stuff your feelings.

Sometimes you will be pushed to the limit in order to realize that you need to take care of yourself.

Do what you can with what you have wherever you are.

———•———

Lead the led life, not the driven life. Live in a relaxed way; there is no need to force things. Strain is not strategy. Driving yourself into the ground through an impossible schedule and over-commitment to activities that drain you will leave you depleted. Let yourself be led and guided to the next steps in your journey.

———•———

Simplify your life and be easy on yourself. You should have a good time doing whatever you are doing. Pace yourself, and make time for fun, rest, and creativity as well as work. No matter what is going on in your life, you still need to enjoy life and have fun.

———•———

Get out of "emergency mode." Some things can wait; life is not an emergency. There is no need to live as though everything is urgent.

———•———

Holidays are just another day of sticking to your self-care plan. Every day is just another day. Every meal is just another meal.

———•———

Any food can be eaten at any time of the day. You can eat steak, chicken, or fish for breakfast. Eat what nourishes your body.

———•———

A self-care program will not be perfect. Just try to be consistent at first. Then make incremental improvements after you master each step.

———•———

Take small chewable chunks to improve at anything.

———•———

Slowing down is a way of being generous with yourself.

———•———

To achieve balance, make small adjustments all the time.

———•———

Self-discipline is self-caring.

———•———

Self-care should be a gentle endeavor, not a military drill. Sometimes you need to take action, but other times you need to do something else to take care of yourself.

———•———

Addictions are a barrier to intimacy because you are not fully present.

Binging on anything strips you of your self-esteem.

Taking on too many activities and responsibilities leads to burnout, depression, and anxiety. The gift of panic attacks is that they slow you down.

You can change the wiring of your brain through practicing new behavior.

Over-functioning is a liability.

Your professional or family life will only be as healthy as you are.

Conscious behavior is often the reverse of unconscious fears.

What you put into your mind creates your attitude every day, which in turn affects your choices and behaviors.

———•———

Are you able to stop spending all of your energy, or do you let your core compulsion keep driving you endlessly? If you stop compulsively using up all of your energy, there will be space for you to be guided by grace.

———•———

Try not to eat your emotions.

———•———

To practice putting ease into your life, eat when you are hungry and rest when you are tired.

———•———

To see if you have balance in your life, write out a time grid of how you really spend your time.

———•———

Impulsiveness is driven by fear.

———•———

Are you taking care of yourself or are you worrying about what other people think of you? Make self-care the top priority in your life. Even if you need to cut out certain things in your life to accommodate your self-care, put it first. It is okay if you cannot do everything you would like to do. Do what you need to do.

———•———

Limiting your food intake is a gift to yourself, not deprivation.

———•———

Stay calm..... Carry on.....

———•———

Rest and sleep are two different things. Have enough self-esteem to allow yourself rest.

———•———

Instead of reaching for something that you should not put in your mouth, ask yourself, "What do I really need right now?"

———•———

Different things work at different times.

———•———

The goal is not to be thin and obsessed; it is about being free.

———•———

Food is not the solution. "Abstinence at any price" means putting abstinence first. Remaining abstinent from certain things does not limit your freedom. It gives you more freedom to enjoy life.

You do not have to do something that is not good for you just because you feel like it. Give up your compulsion to feel comfortable.

Making decisions because they are healthy for you is obedience to the unenforceable.

Savor your food. There is no need to scarf it down.

Go ahead and get rid of things. There is plenty more to come.

Down-time is an important part of self-care.

Acceptance is energy conservation. Strive for radical acceptance of everything.

Listen to the small inner nudges about what to do to take care of yourself next.

Slowness is the key to happiness.

If it is not good for your body, it is not a treat.

An injury is a constant reminder to keep the focus on taking care of yourself.

Self-control gives you the freedom to live up to your full potential.

Overeating and overspending are two ways of punishing and beating yourself up.

Listen to your body and respond to it. Do not ignore what your body is telling you. It is a very intelligent machine capable of enormous healing.

Taking care of yourself leads to feeling grateful and generous.

———•———

Stay in self-care. Overworking and being exhausted lead to making foolish choices. Keep a balance between attending to responsibilities in service to others and self-care.

———•———

Putting self-discipline into action will allow your creativity to flow and the internal chaos to dissipate.

———•———

The more self-care activities you engage in the more energy you will have.

———•———

The way you take care of yourself will give you a feeling of abundance that money cannot give you.

———•———

In order to connect with your soul and God, meditate. It allows you to detach with love from your own mind. Try to meditate for at least ten minutes daily. The regular practice of meditation reduces reactivity and gives you emotional balance and the ability to respond productively and intuitively to situations that you previously could not handle. It will allow you to connect with people and the world at a higher level.

———•———

Overeating, overdrinking, overworking, and becoming overtired are forms of self-abuse.

———•———

Part of physical self-care involves having clothes and shoes that are sized correctly to fit your body.

———•———

Plan and pace yourself. Everything does not have to be done in one day.

———•———

Weigh and measure your time, energy, and food.

———•———

Time and repetition will help you to reprogram unhealthy habits.

———•———

The sweet life wins over the sweet taste. If sugar is a problem, let it go.

———•———

When you start to feel anxious, physically slow down and relax your body. The feeling will pass.

———•———

You may come to a healthy self-care routine for the vanity, but you will stay for the sanity.

———

The more you fear, the less you relax. The more you relax, the less you fear.

———

First do your self-care routine every day. Then fit the rest of your life around it.

———

Even if you have bad judgment, good habits will bail you out.

———

If it is moderate behavior, you can stop it yourself. If it is problem behavior, you can stop it with help from others. If it is an addiction, you need spiritual help in addition to human help. Addictions are characterized by obsession, compulsion, denial, withdrawal, craving, and distortion of the truth.

———

Gratitude is the integrating force for healing body, mind, and spirit.

———

Keep time boundaries by not pushing past your own body's limits. For example, rest when you are tired, eat when you are hungry, and go to bed on time.

———•———

Food is not defined by what that tastes good. It is something that nourishes your body. Choose food that will strengthen your body and nurture your soul instead of food that will leave you with emotional despair, mental fog, and lethargy. Give time and attention to planning and preparing your meals.

———•———

If you have a problem with eating cookies, decide that you are worth more than a cookie. Ask yourself, "What you are really hungry for?" Eating something will not really provide love, companionship, or peace.

———•———

Everyone has limitations. Stop when your body says to stop.

———•———

Face your stuff or stuff your face.

———•———

Being overworked or overtired can lead to overindulging.

———•———

Attending to your nutrition reflects a belief that you deserve to feel good.

———•———

If you deprive yourself, you are more likely to binge later.

———•———

Back pain can be the manifestation of resentment and anger.

———•———

Recognize and respect the limits of your body and energy.

———•———

Eat responsibly. There is no need to have a party in your mouth.

———•———

Chronic stress can make you chronically exhausted.

———•———

You can get through any health problem by telling yourself daily, "Just for today, I am healthy and happy," or "Right now, I am okay."

———•———

Physical self-care improves mental and spiritual conditions.

———•———

Maintaining and adhering to a plan of eating that nurtures your body is the highest form of self-love. Eating poorly can be a way of depriving and punishing yourself.

———•———

Greed turns enjoyment into an addiction.

———•———

Mood altering substances keep you from being present. It is either the substance or your life.

———•———

Instead of thinking that someone else is walking too slowly, consider that you may be walking too quickly.

———•———

Make attending to your physical, emotional, and spiritual health your top priority.

———•———

Being physically sick can affect your spiritual condition. Being spiritually sick can also affect your physical condition.

———•———

When you start to feel crazy, get back to the business of self-care.

———•———

Life is not urgent. Slow down. Other people cannot stress you out, only you can do that to yourself. Be gentle with yourself. If you think things are going too slowly, then you need to slow down.

———•———

Accepting the aging process is part of humility.

———•———

Going into external organizing behaviors can help when you feel like you lack internal organization.

———•———

Do you care enough about yourself to attend to your basic self-care? If you do small things to take care of yourself daily, such as sleep, nourishment, social support, and exercise, then the big picture will take care of itself.

———•———

Try not to skip sleep or miss a meal for someone else's sake.

———•———

Try self-control instead of self-sacrifice. If you are able to implement moderation with food and manage the quantities and frequency of consumption, there is no food you cannot eat.

———

To break destructive patterns in your life, examine your perceptions and why you want to change. Then find a mechanism to break the negative cycle, form good habits, detox yourself of any resentment you are carrying, and surround yourself with supportive people who will help you stay focused.

———

If you can keep yourself relaxed, you can let in the goodness of every day.

———

Be careful of what you reach for when you are lonely.

———

Pay attention to your needs and to what your body is telling you before you reach a crisis point.

———

Treat yourself kindly in the midst of upheavals in your life.

———

When you are tired, sometimes you will gain more energy by going out and connecting with others than by sleeping.

———•———

If you are sleep-deprived, the first thing that is impaired is your judgment.

———•———

God will speak to you through your body.

———•———

Take one day a week to focus on taking care of yourself through rest, prayer, meditation, exercise, and fun.

———•———

Habits can be broken.

———•———

Take one half hour of quiet time every day to be still.

———•———

It is more about how you feel than how you look.

———•———

Taking care of yourself does not mean you have to do it by yourself. Ask for help.

———•———

Meditation is like medication. It changes your brain chemistry and improves mood and overall functioning.

———•———

Sometimes being sick is a manifestation of internalizing a negative or unhealthy environment.

———•———

Appreciate your abilities to do simple things to take care of yourself like driving, brushing your teeth, eating, exercising, working, and getting dressed.

———•———

Physical problems can be a message to slow down.

———•———

It is not necessary to do it all.

———•———

Be willing to let go of anything that stands in the way of your health.

———•———

Take the time and space you need to recharge your batteries.

When you do not feel well, lower your standards for yourself and just focus on taking care of yourself.

Being more physically active can help to pull you out of depression.

Cultivate self-care as your top priority.

Listen to your instincts about what to do to take care of yourself.

Continue to exercise your mind so that you can continue to grow and improve your life.

What is your plan for eating the right foods and getting enough rest?

Eat to live instead of living to eat.

———•———

You have a choice about whether you want to feel relaxed or tense. Go a little slower, and just focus on the task at hand.

———•———

If you are tired, forget everything else and take care of yourself.

———•———

Have time boundaries around self-care such as eating on time, starting and ending the workday on time, and getting to bed on time.

———•———

It is never all going to be done. There will always be something left unfinished. Decide how much is good enough so that you can enjoy the present moment.

———•———

If you do the simple basics to take care of yourself, you will have serenity and joy in your life no matter what is going on. The basics are exercise, sleep, nutrition, spiritual practices, social support, medical care, and mental health care.

———•———

5
SELF-ESTEEM

With wraparound support, you can do anything.

———•———

Valuing yourself helps you to be able to reach out to others and be of service.

———•———

The biggest stumbling blocks to building character are pride, insecurity, moodiness, perfectionism, oversensitivity, and negativity.

———•———

Integrity involves being the same person regardless of who you are with, making choices for the greater good rather than from selfishness, and keeping your commitments.

———•———

You are responsible to decorate your own life.

———•———

Freedom comes from paying your own way. It is not necessary to feel dependent upon or indebted to people.

———•———

If someone's behavior is detrimental to you, you have a choice about whether or not to be around them. You can be available to yourself by being unavailable to them.

———•———

Move the distractions out of the way, and go for what you really want.

———•———

Honesty begins with "I want," or "I don't want to..."

———•———

It is basically up to you to figure out what you want and then do something about it.

———•———

You can be a victim or a creator. As a creator, you take control and responsibility.

———•———

Things are not good or bad. The question is whether something is working for you.

———•———

Most decisions are not big, bold, well thought-out decisions. They happen for small reasons that accumulate and gradually guide you to more significant decisions.

———•———

Think for yourself. Just because someone says something does not make it true.

———•———

Although you may have no control over making others treat you differently, you can treat yourself differently.

———•———

Instead of focusing on what is missing or what is lacking from your life, focus on what you want and bring that into your life.

———•———

Strive for constant incremental improvement. It is difficult to improve if you do the same things, the same way every day. Try something new.

———•———

Some people need to stand up, and some people need to sit down.

———•———

It is not vain to attend to your appearance; it reflects a healthy-self-esteem and is human.

———•———

Let go of trying to force yourself to change. All you have to do is show up and be willing. When you are ready, the changes will happen.

———•———

Speak your mind.

———•———

It is not selfish to do what you enjoy.

———•———

Whenever you make a person, place, or situation too important, things can backfire on you. Have boundaries and balance.

———•———

The way to change your patterns is through action rather than waiting for your attitude to change.

———•———

You have to deal with all the things in your life, even the things that are difficult. Give up cutting things out of your life that really do matter.

———•———

Let your feelings inform you of what you need to know. Instead of being other- directed and looking for the answers from people, listen to yourself. This is a form of taking responsibility for yourself.

———•———

Do what you really want to do with your time and energy instead of forcing yourself to do things that do not serve you.

———•———

Perfectionism can make you focus on one bad thing when many other good things are happening.

———•———

When you get anxious, just try to walk through the situation. Tell yourself you have walked through many other things before, and you can walk through this one too.

———•———

You can act with courage even when you are afraid.

———•———

Rather than trying to rigidly control your feelings, use them to lead and guide you.

———•———

It is not what happens that is important; it is how you handle what happens that is important.

———•———

Following all the rules all the time can be based on fear.

———•———

The world is a fluid place. Even if you make a decision, you can always change your mind. There are very few decisions in life that cannot be modified.

———•———

Learn to express what you really feel. Always being pleasant is not authentic.

———•———

You are entitled to a life, and you are supposed to enjoy it.

———•———

Look at your own being and who you are being.

———•———

Part of maturity is the realization that other people's approval is not your authority. Self-worth does not come from other people's approval. It comes from loving yourself and making choices in your own best interest.

———•———

Let go of the feelings that others are out to get you. Most people really do wish you well. The rest are probably neutral.

———•———

It is not always possible to figure out and explain the way it used to be. You just need to say to yourself that "That's the way it was...," move on, and figure out what you need to do next to take care of yourself.

———•———

Trust what you know, see, and feel.

———•———

Do something with your life. Do not tolerate a life that you do not want.

———•———

Valuing yourself as important does not downgrade the other person. Discern what you need, and nurture yourself.

———•———

Rely on yourself, not others, to make you feel good about yourself.

———•———

Low self-esteem can keep you from realizing that you have an impact on other people without knowing it.

———•———

Anger can be used to motivate you or to protect you from other people.

———•———

When you do things you never thought you could do, it frees you of your dependencies on other people.

———•———

Giving yourself what you want can be a source of your abundance.

———•———

To overcome your shortcomings, you need to first know what they are. Practice regular self-examination. To get going in the right direction, you need to know where you have been.

———•———

In order to accept yourself, you have to know yourself.

———•———

Avoid letting insignificant things rule your life.

———•———

Fear and anxiety creep in when you stop taking care of yourself.

———•———

You do not control people or circumstances outside of you, but they do not control you either. You are in control of your own thoughts, life, and perspective.

———•———

Another person does not have to change for your life to get better.

———•———

Inheritance is not destiny. Break your dysfunctional family patterns.

———•———

Stop shortchanging yourself by putting your needs last.

———•———

Reach out to others daily to avoid social anorexia.

———•———

When you are struggling, do something kind and gentle for yourself instead of pushing yourself even harder.

———•———

Be more fluid and less rigid.

———•———

Self-responsibility is freedom, which allows you to move from victimhood into trying new behaviors and getting new results.

———•———

Ask yourself every day what actions you can take to create something positive in your life.

———•———

There is an asset waiting to shine behind every character problem.

———•———

If you are uncomfortable with your old behavior, then you are already moving towards changing it.

———•———

Other people's energy and beliefs do not have to distract you from your own.

———•———

If you are in a bad situation, ask yourself, "What am I supposed to learn from this?"

———•———

When there is no clear answer to something, the answer is to not do anything. When you are not sure what to do, sit still, do less, and let things work themselves out.

———•———

Boundaries are about what you DO want, and expressing it.

———•———

Your self-esteem will grow when you stop acting like a victim and stop expecting other people to take care of you.

———•———

Putting people on pedestals will cause you to have unrealistic expectations of them. You will expect them to be something they are not. This tendency comes from a sense of inadequacy and a lack of sense of self. Take people off of their pedestals, stand up, and grow up.

———•———

Before you die, be all that you can be.

———•———

You have control over your own attitudes and actions but not much else.

———•———

Stop turning away from yourself.

———•———

Maintain your own integrity. Just because you sit in a garage does not mean you have to turn into a car.

———•———

Build your life based on what you can do, not based on someone else's moods.

———•———

It is a delusion that you are limited and that you are not able to do more than you are doing now.

———•———

If you are an adult and are still getting victimized, it is your choice. You are an adult now, and you can put a stop to it.

———•———

Your spirit will be set free when you take the risk of self-expression. Be expansive; allow yourself full expression in the world.

———•———

Give up being nice to people who hurt you.

———•———

Boundaries create self-respect and identity.

———•———

Avoiding life can be a form of self-punishment.

———•———

Pursue your passions and things you love. Pursue relationships.

———•———

Replace perfectionism with patience.

———•———

Give up defining yourself by the negative things in your life or by what other people say you cannot do.

———•———

Instead of beating yourself up about the past, ask yourself what your goal is for the next time.

———•———

Not getting angry when you should can be a form of not valuing yourself, lying, and people-pleasing. Expressing your anger appropriately is the key to using it constructively.

———•———

At a certain point of maturity, you need to stop looking for your mom and dad in other people when you are vulnerable, and learn how to take care of yourself.

———•———

Self-love is an antidote to fear.

———•———

Listen to yourself more then you listen to others.

———•———

Stop explaining yourself compulsively.

———•———

Be open to new ideas and directions. Let go of thinking that you must stay the same, stay in your place, and not change.

———•———

Going with the flow means going with your own gut.

———•———

Your integrity depends on going for the desires of your heart.

———•———

Reclaim the things in your life that bring you joy.

———•———

Try not to make things harder than they are. Let go of making big things out of little things by worrying and fretting. If you just stay in the moment, life will be easier and the fear will melt away.

———•———

How much are you driven by the need to prove that you are okay?

———•———

What is your motive for the service that you are doing? Doing too much service to please others can lead to resentment. Have balance and boundaries.

———•———

Are you working or lurking in your life? If you are working, you are engaged in positive growth and change. If you are lurking, you are just hanging around on the sidelines of your life.

———•———

Follow your instincts, rather than what someone else says is right. Are you trying to know yourself or please others? Being dependent on other people's approval is a form of living in bondage to approval addiction.

———•———

The tiny voice inside that says, "I might like to do X..." tells you what your heart's desires are.

———•———

Cherish your happiness, not your wounded-ness.

———•———

Letting go of perfectionism means that you can arrive late for something if you have a good reason.

———•———

Reflect a high regard for yourself by not attending every argument that you are invited to.

———•———

It is always okay to choose to change your mind.

———•———

Stop running away from people who are good for you.

———•———

Be discerning. It is not necessary to tell everybody everything you are doing, what you are feeling or to answer every question that you are asked.

———•———

Lightness of being comes from living for yourself. Release yourself from the burden of falsely-held responsibilities. You are probably not responsible for ninety percent of what you worry about and try to control.

———•———

You do not have to look, act, or be a certain way in order to make it in life.

To change your character, practice having a different response.

If someone brings up a subject you would rather not discuss, use distraction to change the topic.

You create your own happiness and misery. They are not the result of other people's choices.

Be accurate, not precise. Do the best you can; it does not have to be perfect.

Just because someone close to you hates their life does not mean that you have to hate your life.

Only say out loud what you want to be true.

Sometimes you need to surrender, and sometimes you need to stand up for yourself. If you are in a toxic situation, do not surrender. You may need to leave.

———•———

Draw a circle around your feet. That is what you are responsible for.

———•———

Find out what you like and love, and do it. What do you do that you really love? What do you want to do? Are you doing what you are doing because somebody else wants you to do it, or because you want to do it? Live your own life, and let other people live theirs.

———•———

What do you want to be in relation to what your parents wanted you to be?

———•———

Living life guided by intellect over emotions is the difference between living a manageable rather than an unmanageable life and reflects the ability to act in your own best interest.

———•———

Try not to battle with people when they are in their own dysfunction. You can still have a good day because of what you are doing for yourself, even if others do not overcome their issues.

———•———

Let go of trying to decipher other people's motives and agendas. Just focus on what you want.

———•———

It is not about what the world can see; it is about matching your insides to your outsides.

———•———

Run with the other horses. Avoid being risk-averse and isolated.

———•———

Go after your joy, not your safety. If you always focus on the negative side of things, you will not want to do them. Instead of living to protect yourself from the negative, go for what you really want.

———•———

Give up being harsh with yourself.

———•———

Do not believe everything you think. Your opinions and judgments are often wrong.

———•———

Do your homework. Trusting blindly and not researching are forms of self-neglect and self-deprivation.

Avoid going towards the pain.

Cultivate a circle of people around you who add value to your life instead of people who cost you too much energy, effort, or time.

If you are not sure what you enjoy, ask yourself what makes you feel as excited as a child.

Making a contribution to things strengthens your internal core.

Speak up for yourself. Not talking about what is really going on is a form of self-deprivation.

Being financially self-supporting gives you the gifts of freedom and independence.

Stay with what is available instead of having a rage because you have been rejected. Step back and make another choice.

It is not your job to be there for people when they are not good for you.

———•———

Sometimes you do not need to want to do something; you just need to be willing to do it.

———•———

Nothing is too extravagant if it makes you happy.

———•———

Rigidity is rooted in fear and leaves no room for error. Avoiding rigidity allows for fluctuation and change.

———•———

Keep opening yourself up to change so that you will not get stuck. Change is supposed to keep happening.

———•———

Stay in the center of your own life.

———•———

Let go of being shame-based. You do not need to automatically assume that you have done something wrong when things go wrong.

———•———

Foolish consistency is the substance of little minds.

———•———

The deal has to serve both of you.

———•———

Your capacity for everything is larger than you think.

———•———

Avoid letting others distract, interrupt, or cause you to drop what you are doing.

———•———

Do one thing at a time. Focus on the thing you are actually doing. If you are driving, drive. If you are speaking, speak. If you are listening, listen.

———•———

Find yourself instead of trying to prove yourself.

———•———

Do not let anyone dump their garbage on you by saying that what you want to do is hard.

———•———

Sometimes you will not be able to do everything. Just do what you can.

What is primary in your life? Is the way you are spending your time consistent with this purpose?

Retain some of your energy rather than giving it all away. Find ways to make your life easier.

There are two good reasons not to do something: 1.You cannot do it; 2.You do not want to do it. Just say no.

What other people want can make you insane if you ignore what you want.

Your heart's desire is whatever keeps trying to get your attention.

If you give yourself over to the distractions in your life, it will be difficult to be happy. Give the distractions the attention they deserve, but stay focused on what makes you happy and balanced.

Every day, wake up and ask yourself what you are afraid of doing that day. Then do it. This will build up your confidence.

———•———

When you work every day on building a new consciousness, it will manifest in new changes in your life.

———•———

Taking care of yourself is the antidote to feeling like a victim.

———•———

You can forgive without opening yourself up to being harmed again. If you can take care of yourself around toxic people, you can love and enjoy them safely and appreciate what they DO give you.

———•———

It is not necessary to continually prove yourself over and over again.

———•———

Focusing on what is good in your life is an important part of living fully.

———•———

Are you a reflection of someone else, or are you rooted in your own identity?

Live your own life and God will support it.

If someone is really toxic for you, be brief, be firm, and be gone.

Being fully self-supporting gives you a sense of safety in the world.

Discomfort with success can cause you to interrupt your own applause.

If you want to know what your dreams are, ask yourself what you would do if time and money were no object.

Pay attention to the obvious things going on.

Feel it, speak it, know it, and show it.

You are not defined by your relationships. You are an individual. The other person is an individual. What you cultivate together is its own thing.

———•———

You do not need to wait for another person to be with you in order to do the things you want to do in your life.

———•———

You can be happy even if other people do not change. You may be waiting for other people to change because you want them to meet your needs. The real solution is for you to meet your own needs or look for your needs to be met from people who can actually do it because they have it to give.

———•———

The person who has abandoned you the most is you.

———•———

Your primary duty to yourself is to live up to your potential. You can reach your goals if you work for them, even if it takes longer than you planned. One you reach a goal, your potential will expand again.

———•———

Let go of adapting to other people's values and be who you are. If you become a chameleon, they may dislike you for it.

Spending money is not just for survival. It is about feeling good about life. Spending that meets your real needs is a form of self-nurture.

If someone is unkind to you, it is their problem. It does not mean that there is something wrong with you.

Being okay with imperfection IS perfection. There is freedom and fun in messiness.

It is not personal when you hear the word "no."

Being authentic means telling the truth about who you are and how you feel, expressing your needs and desires, and asking for what you want.

There is only one human being who can inhabit your body.

When you become impatient or unreasonable, you have probably taken on more than you can handle.

———•———

If you are in a system that is not working, just go ahead and take care of yourself.

———•———

Your attitude determines your altitude.

———•———

Asserting yourself is a form of self-care. Avoid letting things build up until you explode and look crazy.

———•———

No one can fix you, control your emotions, or tell you what you should do. You need to do these things for yourself with support and help. The most that other people can do is to help you help yourself.

———•———

Thinking that something is your fault when it is not is a form of inappropriate responsibility. It is based on the illusion that you had some control over it in the first place.

———•———

Say what you need whether you get it or not.

———•———

Cultivate an accurate picture of yourself. Not examining yourself is like driving up a one way street and just pulling over and sitting there. You need to go back and look at where you went wrong and what you did right. It is important to make peace with your past in order to live comfortably.

———•———

What are your heart's desires for your life?

———•———

Evaluate your loyalties and decide if they are serving you well.

———•———

Having money in savings is an act of self-esteem.

———•———

Let go of taking other people's burdens on your shoulders.

———•———

Seek advice, but trust your instincts in the end. They will tell you what is best for you.

———•———

It is enough that you get it. Everyone else does not have to.

———•———

Realize your intrinsic worth; value is spiritual. It is not necessarily linked to effort or money.

———•———

Refusing to react too quickly to others is a form of self-respect.

———•———

The person that you are in relationship with the most is yourself. Look at the mirror instead of the microscope.

———•———

When you change, things around you change.

———•———

Exchange role-playing for reality. This means being who you really are instead of who you think you are supposed to be. Is your life what you want or what someone else wants? Be the author of your own story. No one else has the authority to define your reality and your life.

———•———

You do not need to say "yes" just because there is a need. Whether you can do something is not as important as whether you want to do something. Avoid doing for others what they can do for themselves.

———•———

Willfulness is a source of misery. Holding others responsible for your misery is the same as holding them responsible for your happiness. Let go of magical thinking and take responsibility for your own happiness instead of waiting for someone to come along and save or fix you.

———•———

Minimize your involvement with people and situations that cause you emotional wear and tear.

———•———

Avoid letting yourself be confined by anyone.

———•———

When you are faced with a decision and do not know which choice to make, do the thing that you will regret the most if you have not done it.

———•———

Making amends with others in rooted in self-love. It removes guilt, shame, and self-loathing.

———•———

Trying to do too much in too little time is a form of thinking you are not enough.

———•———

Acting out is deserting yourself.

———

The greatest amend you can make to yourself is to keep a positive focus.

———

Take care of both the inside and the outside of your life.

———

You can have more peace by making small, positive choices.

———

Minding your own business is a full-time job.

———

What other people think of you does not define you.

———

Be with people who feed your soul rather than people who feed off of you.

———

Give yourself a break when you do not know how to handle a situation. There is no situation so bad that beating yourself up will not make it worse.

—•—

The only real truth is how you feel about something.

—•—

Your own actions determine your self-worth. It is not defined by others.

—•—

Stick with your own opinions even when people around you have differing opinions. Sometimes it is better to say nothing or that you have no opinion about something.

—•—

Be the principal player in your own life.

—•—

Love yourself without getting trapped in the bondage of self.

—•—

Be your own person, tell the truth, and get out from behind the façade.

—•—

Value yourself without pretending to be more or less than you are.

———+———

Self-acceptance involves the realization that there is nothing wrong with you exactly the way you are and that there never was.

———+———

Even when you are powerless over other people, you still have a lot of choices you can make for yourself.

———+———

The really good stuff in life is not what others give you, but what you give yourself.

———+———

If it is too hot, put it down.

———+———

If it is not yours, do not pick it up.

———+———

Give yourself the love that you think others should give you.

———+———

Listen to your inner voice and intuition, not just your head and logic. If something does not feel right to you, listen and do not do it. Avoid letting your mind talk you into it. Trust your feelings more than your mind or your thinking.

———•———

Speak your truth.

———•———

Instead of saying "yes" when you want to say "no," say "yes" when you want to say "yes," and say "no" when you want to say "no."

———•———

When faced with difficult situations or decisions, recognize that you are doing the best you can. Do your best, and then let it go.

———•———

Your opinion of yourself should come from you. If you base your confidence on what other people think of you, you are giving up your power. You do not have to wait for other people's approval to feel good about yourself.

———•———

Avoid letting what you do depend on what others are doing.

———•———

Just be yourself without worrying so much about fitting in. Be less constricted.

———•———

Choose to do the thing that will take the best care of you.

———•———

Relying too much on others' opinions can lead to self-doubt. You will usually make the right decisions if you listen to your inner self.

———•———

It is more important that you express how you feel rather than that which the other person understands.

———•———

Be open to new ideas. It is perfectly acceptable for you to change your mind about anything, at any time.

———•———

No one can take away your joy without your permission.

———•———

Share your secrets. Keeping secrets can lead you into emotional and spiritual isolation.

———•———

Rather than seeking perfection, learn to be good enough without having any regrets.

The power you have is the power to be you. What defines your identity? Do you introduce yourself as someone's child or spouse or by your own name?

Your parents might have been the reason you started out the way you did, but it is your responsibility if you stay that way.

Accept that when someone gives you a compliment, it is true. All you need to do to respond is to stay still, smile, and say, "Thank you."

If it is easier for you to feel bad than to feel good, then you may be addicted to suffering.

When you are wrong, simply admit it. Period. Then move on and take corrective action without beating yourself up. This will keep you in good working condition, so that you are not weighed down with unnecessary burdens. We all make mistakes every day. If you do not let them accumulate, you will travel lightly and more joyously. Be gentle with yourself. When a grocer takes an inventory of his store, he does not rage and freak out because he does not have enough peas. He simply gets more peas. Do the same thing with yourself, and be kind to yourself. If you are going to beat yourself up, use a feather, not a bat.

Trusting your intuition will tell you the truth about your reality. Stick with your own reality, but also take into account the feelings of others. Self-love is not about being totally selfish.

Take people off of their pedestals. Seeking other's approval can be a form of self-abandonment and giving up your power to other people.

As long as you do not hurt other people, run your own life as you see fit. Other people cannot determine who you are, how you feel, or what you need.

Take the space that you need to be where you need to be. It is not required that you get anyone's permission, just take it.

In order to love yourself today, let go of the past.

"God, give me the courage to change the only person I can and the wisdom to know it's me."

———•———

You are the one who generates your own experience, including your, happiness, responses to things and the quality of your life. Other people do not need to get their act together for you to be happy. Be self-defining.

———•———

If you let your day be ruined by someone else's anger, your self-esteem is running low.

———•———

What is good for you is good for everybody around you. Keep the focus on taking care of yourself, because when you are miserable, everybody else is miserable.

———•———

If you are going to be lonely, you might as well do it by yourself. It can be much lonelier to be with someone that you cannot connect with than to actually be alone.

———•———

Self-love is about not taking on more than you can handle and giving yourself some breathing room.

———•———

You need to be on your own side before you can expect anyone else to be.

———•———

The most painful loss is the loss of self.

———•———

When you are feeling raw and vulnerable, there are certain places you should not go to and certain people you should not call. This is discernment; it is not being judgmental. Go to people who can nurture you and give you what you need.

———•———

Choose the type of person you want to become.

———•———

If you are walking around feeling like something is missing in your life, then that something is you.

———•———

Your life belongs to you. You have a right to your life. You are not just here to make other people feel good.

———•———

Who you are is who you have chosen to be.

———•———

Put your serenity ahead of everything else.

———•———

The healthy boundaries that you have with other people are a measure of your self-respect. Limit your exposure to people who are toxic for you through portion control.

———•———

Just because someone asks you for something does not mean you have to do it. You can say, "no," or "yes," or "maybe," or "not right now." Know the limits of what you can and cannot do. It is okay to just say "no" to something because it will not work. You do not have to explain yourself to others out of guilt or to try to make them feel comfortable.

———•———

Let go of feeling guilty or embarrassed about taking care of yourself. It is okay to take care of yourself and do what is best for you as long as you do not harm anyone else.

———•———

As people mature and grow, they begin to give themselves the love they were always looking for others to give them.

———•———

On your birthday or another special occasion, be proactive and plan something for yourself that you will enjoy. Holidays and birthdays are not about other people doing things for you. Celebrate these days by doing things for yourself. It is not always realistic to expect others to serve you and know what you want.

———•———

You are equal to everyone else. Low self-esteem is at the root of the exact nature of many wrongs.

———•———

Give yourself the very simple things that you like.

———•———

Give yourself permission to examine and ask yourself what you really want.

———•———

First you learn that you do not fit in. Then you learn that it is okay not to fit in. Then you learn that you do not want to fit in.

———•———

Building a life happens in baby steps. What do you need to do for self-care? What is fun for you? Who makes you feel good about yourself? What clear boundaries do you need to set in order to maintain your focus? Part of self-love is to not allow yourself to be distracted from what you know you need to do.

Practicing good behavior allows you to have confidence and stand up straight.

———•———

Self-love is the nourishment that makes everything good in your life flourish.

———•———

You have three characters: 1. What you think you are, 2. What you want others to think you are, and 3. What you really are.

———•———

When receiving input from others, take what you like and leave the rest.

———•———

Minding someone else's business is a form of self-abandonment. It can be a way of avoiding your own loneliness.

———•———

If you are hard on yourself, you will be hard on other people.

———•———

Holding on to the past keeps you from moving forward.

———•———

Taking care of your own needs keeps you free and independent. Let go of trying to get people to rescue you.

———•———

Can you live with yourself if you take this action? Can you live with yourself if you do not take this action?

———•———

Taking yourself too seriously hurts your perspective on what you can accomplish in your life. There is a time to be serious and a time to be light.

———•———

Let go of shame. Shame is an acronym for "should have already mastered everything."

———•———

Meeting your own needs works more effectively than trying to get your needs met through other people. You do not need other people's approval to meet your own needs. Just go ahead and do it.

———•———

Be neither harnessed nor harassed by the opinions of others.

———•———

Difficulties with proportion have to do with balance and boundaries.

———•———

You are a combination of three things: who you think you are, who you want other people to think you are, and who you really are.

———•———

Keeping things simple involves not taking on too much or complicating things too much. Learn to say "no" and turn things over to other people when appropriate.

———•———

Exercise your choices. Make whatever decisions are in your best interest provided that you are not harming anyone else. Respect other people's right to do the same and make their own decisions. Only give them advice if they ask for it, otherwise you may be criticizing them without realizing it.

———•———

Other people's opinions are not more important than your own.

———•———

Instead of waiting for someone to come along and love you, start by learning to love yourself.

———•———

Allow yourself to make a mistake. You do not need to be amazing all the time.

———•———

Just because someone gives you feedback does not mean you have to take it. If you ask for it, take it. Otherwise, consider the source.

———•———

Do what you need to do, but also do what you want to do.

———•———

Identify what you need, then take responsibility for getting it.

———•———

You possess the same fine qualities that you admire in others. If the quality is not in you, you would not see it in them. If you spot it, you have got it.

———•———

Instead of choosing people, places, and situations that bring excitement into your life, try to choose people, places, and situations that bring ease into your life.

———•———

Find the middle ground between being too big and too small.

Let go of trying to become who you think other people want you to be. Authenticity comes from being yourself and living honestly.

Continually shake things off yourself by talking, writing, or taking action.

When faced with a difficult decision, ask yourself what is in your best interest and what will enable you to like yourself later.

Other people cannot tell you how to live your life.

Minding your own business is setting a boundary.

Spread out your dependency needs. No one person can give you everything.

Be willing to let go of old attitudes and behaviors in order to make room for better ones.

———•———

It is more important to be alive and relaxed than to look good.

———•———

When something is going on inside you, identify it, accept it, and do something about it.

———•———

Take the information you have, and follow your heart.

———•———

Use the following tools to detach and to avoid taking on other people's issues: "Let's talk about this later," or "I don't think I'll get involved in this," or "Let me get back to you on this."

———•———

You can be who you want to be without being who you have always been. Are you being loyal to your old self?

———•———

How do you like your own eggs cooked? The answer should not depend on who you are with.

—•—

Consistency is integrity; it is being true to oneself.

—•—

Is it good enough for now?

—•—

Living in extremes keeps you from being in balance. Guard against being either too wild or too repressed.

—•—

No action is too small to change your spirit.

—•—

Nobody can make you do or feel anything.

—•—

Speaking up for yourself prevents resentment.

—•—

Set yourself up so that you can enjoy family holiday visits. Do not be too rigid about your schedule. Take time out to rest and relax, do not get overtired, and allow others to help you.

—•—

Wear the world like a loose garment, and have fun.

———•———

Back away from whatever feels wrong, and focus on living your life to the fullest.

———•———

Be gentle with yourself, take it easy, and enjoy the moments.

———•———

It is okay to say "no" to something because you cannot handle it. Sometimes you have to say "no" to something in order to say "yes" to something else.

———•———

Become who you really are instead of who you think you are supposed to be.

———•———

Try to be aware of your own needs, and do all you can to meet them.

———•———

Do things that enhance your self-esteem, like having relationships with people who really care about you.

———•———

If you lose your peace, you lose your joy. If you lose your joy, you lose your strength.

———•———

If you focus on your own needs first, you will have more to give others.

———•———

It is up to you to take responsibility for yourself and ask for the help you need in every area of your life.

———•———

Give yourself permission to make mid-course corrections. You do not have to get it right the first time.

———•———

When you stop being secretive, shame lifts, and you begin to heal.

———•———

Do things because you want to do them, not because other people want you to do them.

———•———

Are you living your own life, or are you living through the lives of others?

———•———

Instead of criticizing others, focus on living your own life to the fullest.

———•———

Valuing yourself: refusing to take offense easily, being kind and open, letting go of resentment, expanding and opening up your universe, sharing yourself, letting people in, putting your well-being first, choosing positive thoughts, taking it easy, stopping to ask yourself what you really want to do, not putting yourself in situations that are not good for you, not explaining and defending yourself, and listening to your feelings before responding.

———•———

6
PROSPERITY

Prosperity is not just about money, although you need enough money to live well. It is about love, relationships, emotional well-being, developing your talents, and living up to your full potential.

———•———

You are enough. You have enough. You do enough.

———•———

What you love will guide you towards your assignment in life. What would you do if time and money were of no concern? What do you love doing so much that you would do it for free? This is your calling.

———•———

Goals are necessary to continue to build character and faith. If you have no goals, your goal is to drift along and stay the same.

———•———

When you are passionately living out your purpose for life, your attitude towards time will change. You will no longer waste any time. You will operate with clarity, focus, and direction.

———•———

Time is the boundary of opportunity.

———•———

Living and surviving are two different things.

———•———

Love every single thing that you own. If you do not love it, get rid of it.

———•———

It is innate for humans to seek increase. The desire for wealth is a desire for a more abundant life.

———•———

What is right under your nose that you have not tapped?

———•———

If you want to learn how to do something, just start doing it.

———•———

The difference between a goal and a fantasy is that you actually work towards a goal. If you are not working on it, it is a fantasy.

———•———

A job needs to be a means of giving service, not a vehicle for accumulating money. Let money be your servant, not your master. It is just a means of exchanging energy with others.

———•———

Fear of financial insecurity is not the same thing as financial insecurity. When the fear of financial insecurity lessens, everything else in life will change.

———•———

If it helps you to promote your business, go ahead and buy it.

———•———

You have sufficient assets. It is your behavior that prevents you from living a full life.

———•———

What you want is already there for you. Just step up and take it.

———•———

Live in the present. Being afraid of spending money and focusing only on savings is a way of living in the wreckage of the future.

———•———

If you did not have to worry about money, what would you do with your time?

———•———

When someone owes you money, be pleasant and try to foster cooperation instead of arguing.

———•———

Time-debting is time mismanagement. Time is the only resource you have that cannot be replaced. What is the best use of your time? Treasure it.

———•———

There is no need to spend a lot of time on something that you dislike or cannot do when you can pay someone else to do it.

———•———

True success is inner fulfillment.

———•———

Clarity gives you the ability to have visions for your life.

———•———

Money is energy.

———•———

It feels good to have integrity, to be above board and to avoid sneaking around. Cheating is often fueled by a sense of inadequacy.

———•———

Paying your own way is a sign of maturity.

———•———

Do not allow yourself to drop the ball because of fear of success.

———•———

You can have a setback yet still keep moving forward. Nine out of ten times, things will work out if you persevere.

———•———

Strive for clarity about the state of your affairs. Vagueness leads to stagnation and numbness.

———•———

If you feel that you have to buy something NOW, you may be acting out of compulsion.

———•———

Taking care of what you already have is a key to inviting more abundance in to your life.

———•———

Financial security does not equal financial serenity.

———•———

Save money, but also spend enough to have a balanced and abundant life.

Following through is a key to prosperity.

Keep your visions big but your steps small.

If you want to experience abundance in some area of your life, talk abundance, think abundance, and act in ways that will increase your abundance. Think positively.

Rule # 1: Show up and try.

It is profitable to just be yourself.

The ultimate goal in life is the ability to fully enjoy what you have.

Allow abundance to come into your life in order to overcome a deprivation mentality.

Are you spending money instead of getting a life?

———•———

Stop throwing money at things that are going to cost you more money in the long run. Buy a new one instead.

———•———

Give up the "nickel and dime" mentality.

———•———

Abundance means having more than you need.

———•———

Let go of wanting something for nothing, looking for the easy way out, or trying to cut corners.

———•———

Fear of success is rooted in codependency. It is okay to be better than other people at something.

———•———

Being of service to others is lucrative. You get back much more than you give.

———•———

Use what you have, or get rid of it. If you are not using what you have, you are wasting it.

———•———

Abundance is the good you do for yourself and others. It will not come unless you pay attention to yourself first.

———•———

Charge your fee on the basis of value, not time. Ask for a fair price for your product, as much as you can ask for without doubting yourself.

———•———

When you hire someone, get three quotes in writing.

———•———

The right things come to you when you need them.

———•———

In order for your creativity to flow, loosen up and relax.

———•———

Under-earning is the reverse of greed.

———•———

Worrying about financial security does not give you financial security. Building a prudent reserve does.

———•———

Try to recognize the opportunities that present themselves to you and take them. Avoid pushing opportunities away.

———•———

See the cup as half-full, not half-empty or not completely full. Half-full means there is room for more.

———•———

You have a scarcity mentality if you constantly think there is not enough time, money, or energy when there really is.

———•———

Busy people return calls promptly.

———•———

If you start getting off track, it may be because you are not communicating with enough people. Communicating with others about what is going on in your life can help you to get back to solutions.

———•———

Business plan: love your clients, but let go of those who are too difficult, pay poorly, or drain you of your energy.

———•———

Check your motives, and make sure that you are not operating out of greed.

———•———

You can only get it if you ask for it.

———•———

Balance the income and the investment.

———•———

Being clean and honest with money gives you confidence and increased self-esteem.

———•———

Asking for enough help is a key to success.

———•———

Your abundance will show up when YOU show up.

———•———

Poverty is more about isolation than deprivation.

———•———

When you start making financial amends and contributions, the money starts to follow and your prosperity increases.

———•———

Buy things that will increase in value or bring more prosperity into your life, including more emotional prosperity and more energy. Let go of buying things that will not hold your interest or that fritter away your time, money, or energy.

———•———

Recognize that you have enough and that you can be generous with others.

———•———

A change of season may bring on the desire for shopping. When you are feeling a lack of things in your life, look at all of your belongings and everything that you own. You will recognize all of the abundance that already exists in your life.

———•———

Hoarding is not spending or using what you have. Putting all of your money in savings is hoarding.

———•———

You are supposed to prosper, be successful, and have the things you want in your life.

———•———

Utilize rather than analyze.

———•———

The way you spend your money reflects your values and your life itself.

———•———

It is okay to fail; it is even more important to try to get in the game of life.

———•———

If you keep holding on to your money, it will not keep flowing in.

———•———

Service to others will make you rich.

———•———

True abundance means having an abundant network of people in your life.

———•———

Success in anything requires cooperation and collaboration with others.

———•———

Less is more, and consistency is key.

Time, money, energy, and your contacts are your primary resources.

Money is spiritual energy.

Prosperity is about intentionality, not frugality.

Debting is about making things complicated, tiring, difficult, and expensive for yourself.

Talents often come from where you have been wounded.

Give up trying to be all things to all people. Do one thing and do it well. Stick with what you do best, and do not allow yourself to get sidetracked.

There is a difference between wanting something and creating it.

———•———

Weigh and measure things that are important to you, like money, energy, and time.

———•———

Debting and under-earning are two different things. Debting means that you buy the cow and do not pay for it. Under-earning means that you buy the cow, do not take care of the cow, the cow dies, and then you blame the cow.

———•———

Networking works best when you give something to the other person.

———•———

Suffering is not a requirement of earning money.

———•———

Discern between the least expensive and what the best fit is for what you really want. Spending less is not necessarily better.

———•———

Give up needing to get it right. Just get it going. It is okay to make mistakes; it does not have to be perfect.

———•———

Try not to fill up every moment and bit of space in your life. Get rid of cheap, flimsy, worn-out things that you do not use, fit, or need or things that make you feel deprived and shabby. Ask yourself if what you have is serving you. If not, then what purpose is it serving?

———•———

Let go of spending too much energy playing it safe, protecting yourself, and not taking any risks.

———•———

Joyful service is right livelihood.

———•———

Strive for excellence, not perfection. Striving for perfection is about control.

———•———

It is under-earning to choose clients who require high effort for low return. Choose clients who are low effort for high return. This leads to emotional and financial prosperity.

———•———

Clarity requires rigorous honesty.

———•———

Go for your dreams. In order to fulfill your visions, you must overcome tradition, fear of ridicule, complacency, fatigue, and naysayers.

———•———

The void is where the magic of creativity happens.

———•———

Being a miser keeps your life very small.

———•———

Let go of the idea that your life can begin when you pay something off.

———•———

Prosperity is whatever feels abundant to you. It does not have to fit anyone else's definition.

———•———

It is not necessary to be manipulative or sneaky to get what you want. You can simply ask and plan for it.

———•———

If you live in gratitude, more and more abundance will come into your life.

———•———

Concentrate on doing what is really necessary, and avoid wasting time on what is not essential.

———•———

You can be successful without being productive every single minute of the day.

———•———

Maximize your opportunities each day. For every opportunity you pass up, there is someone else there waiting to jump on it.

———•———

To avoid time-debting and living in hyper-response mode, only check e-mail and voicemail twice a day. Prioritize what needs an immediate response from what can wait.

———•———

When you are at work, spend your time and energy on activities that are revenue-generating.

———•———

Always looking for the cheapest solution leads to deprivation, entitlement, and scarcity thinking.

———•———

Distraction, deception, and ignorance are the three main obstacles to an abundant life.

—•—

Give up the need to fritter away money because you feel deprived. You may be frittering away money on small things because you are not getting the big things you want in life. Save your money for what you really want instead of wasting it on small things.

—•—

Worrying about money is not the same thing as making more money. It does not make you prosperous.

—•—

Time is best spent taking direct action.

—•—

It is not about how much you spend or save. It is about the decision and compulsion behind it.

—•—

Do not answer calls and e-mails when you do not have time to process and respond to them. This is stress-inducing, self-sabotaging behavior.

—•—

There are three types of business goals: fun, fame, and fortune. How do you rank these in order of priority? When you are having fun, fortune and fame take care of themselves.

If you are earning good money but living as though you are impoverished, you may be a deprivation addict.

Have balance with your money. You do not need to keep it all or spend it all. One third can be spent on whatever you want, another third is for basic needs, and another third is to keep.

Allow yourself to shine without feeling as though you need to shrink because you are afraid that others will feel bad if you out-shine them. Dismantling your abundance and prosperity because of the envy of others is a form of codependency and people-pleasing.

Plan your work and work your plan.

To make a request of someone for something you want, say "Hey, would you consider doing X?"

Learn to negotiate; speak what you want without emotion.

———•———

Things that are meant to be yours will come to you. Things that are not meant to be yours will not.

———•———

Sometimes the deals that you do not get are the ones that make you successful.

———•———

Is the short-lived buzz that you get from buying something really worth all the time and effort it took to earn the money to get it?

———•———

A person who makes no mistakes usually makes nothing.

———•———

Overworking is not the path to abundance. How much do you want to work? It is okay to say "no" or that you are not available.

———•———

Plan the actions rather than the results. With the right tools, you can do anything you want to do.

———•———

Let go of the old to make room for the new.

If something does not need to be in your life, you will not get it.

Do things patiently and properly, and let the process be what it needs to be. It can be self-sabotage to try to resolve everything immediately without taking time to investigate and process information.

Prosperous people keep their lives in order, organized and uncluttered. Getting rid of clutter reduces the chaos in your life and in your head.

Your ability to take care of your business is only as good as your self-care.

Strive to continuously upgrade everything about yourself and your life.

The greatest asset is history. The greatest danger is rigidity.

Prosperous people are very intentional about their time and money.

———•———

Take actions based on the internal nudges that you feel.

———•———

The quality of your life is directly proportional to the focus of your attention.

———•———

Build your business around your life instead of building your life around your business.

———•———

Clutter blocks abundance. Learn to be conscious of your possessions. Know and use what you have, including your spiritual talents and gifts. Discard things that are not useful to you, including old attitudes and behaviors. De-cluttering and getting rid of things that no longer serve you can make space in your life for new energy to come in and increase your prosperity.

———•———

Emotional fear can lead to financial fear, which can lead to overworking, which can lead to isolation.

———•———

Failure is not the problem. Not trying is the problem.

———

Experience is what you gain when you do not get what you want.

———

Give your energy out to things that serve you.

———

Cease to be in the audience of life. Your purpose is about more than just applauding others.

———

Abundance is not measured by what you have but by what you can give.

———

If you argue for your limitations, you get to keep them. You can choose to not live according to your old limitations.

———

Feelings of inferiority can drive you to seek more and more and more and more.

———

When you are really busy enjoying your life, you will be too busy for resentment.

———•———

Develop a healthy relationship with money. Allow it to be in your life, feel comfortable with it, and do not push it away, give it away, or spend too much because you feel undeserving of it.

———•———

Being fully self-supporting involves asking for help.

———•———

It is not about how much you have; it is about what you do with what you have.

———•———

Spending too much time on someone else's agenda can sabotage your own prosperity.

———•———

Focus on the abundance in your life, not the lack. This means enjoying what you already have instead of focusing on chronic dissatisfaction and feeling like you do not have enough. Challenge the lie of lack. When you feel deprived, do a written inventory of what you actually have.

———•———

Wanting what you have results in feeling that you have enough.

Trace it, face it, and erase it.

Doing the right thing is easier than juggling or cheating.

Success is giving something your best and then finishing it.

Ask for what you deserve. Believe that you deserve more in your life. It is okay to say, "That is not enough for me," instead of clamming up and getting resentful. It is okay to believe that you deserve more.

You will love your work more if you put yourself first and take care of your basic needs first.

Maintain momentum toward your goals.

So what, now what? What you feel is not always relevant. What are you going to do now?

———•———

Shrinking back when success starts to rear its head is a form of snatching defeat from the jaws of victory.

———•———

If you have it, use it. The biggest sin is waste.

———•———

Cultivate the vision and then create the causes and conditions for the vision to thrive.

———•———

Rushing and not allowing enough time for things is a form of self-debting.

———•———

You can have abundance without killing yourself or overworking. Let it in and recognize what is already there. Are you as aware of all the abundance that already exists in your life as you are of the lack?

———•———

Use and maximize all of your resources, including yourself.

———•———

It is not necessary to continually prove yourself.

Service should be for fun and for free.

Never let your mood stop you from taking the actions you need to take when something needs to be done.

What you bring in to your life is just as important as what you let go.

To live in prosperity means saying "yes" to life.

Set your mind to what you want, ask for help, give it your all, and let go of the results.

The way you do anything is the way you do everything.

The more you set boundaries with time at work, such as leaving on time and taking breaks, the better your performance is.

———•———

Ask and follow up.

———•———

Distractions keep you from focusing on what is most important and what you need to do. Eliminate the energy drains in your life so that you will be able to take the next step towards prosperity.

———•———

Aim to be authentic rather than successful.

———•———

There is enough time.

———•———

Nothing important is urgent. Nothing urgent is important.

———•———

It is not about the money; it is about the way you deal with money.

———•———

Shopping is often about the behavior, not the item. Overspending only gives you the illusion that you have accomplished something; it is not an accomplishment in and of itself. Spending money on excess things will not fix you; it will just give you a temporary high.

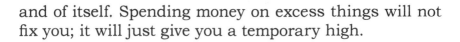

Creative energy flows when you stop misdirecting your time, money, and energy.

There is always going to be something undone or imperfect. It is okay.

Staying small does not keep you safe.

Ask for lots of help so that your success can grow.

Practice truthful behavior.

Look for abundance where you are instead of always seeking it somewhere else.

Having a balanced life means having limits and saying "no" to certain things and "yes" to others.

———•———

What you do with what you know is more important than what you know. Steps of action are more fruitful than knowledge.

———•———

The fact that you are right does not mean things will be resolved on your schedule. They will resolve in their own time.

———•———

Stealing even little things chips away at your self-esteem.

———•———

You can take action without knowing everything beforehand. All you really need to know is enough to get started.

———•———

Try not to let other people's negativity get in the way of your visions and dreams. This is a form of people-pleasing. Go to any length to follow your vision, and avoid the naysayers. If you really believe and make a commitment to doing something in the world, the universe will usually conspire to help you. When you truly commit to your vision, small miracles will occur that help to make it happen. It will be delivered.

———•———

Take the actions you need to take to do what is necessary.

———•———

Giving away or stifling your spirit, time, money, or power can be under-earning, a form of self-deprivation and self-jailing that results in living an anorexic "half- life."

———•———

Not making a choice is a choice.

———•———

Your past mistakes will not be held against you if you change for the better now.

———•———

Try to build up the prosperity of goodwill from those you come in contact with. Brilliance is not enough to get by. Goodwill from others brings you abundance.

———•———

Maintain a balance between saving for the future and living for today.

———•———

What can be changed? What must you accept? If it cannot be changed, leave it alone.

———•———

The way you spend your money reflects your life and values.

———•———

If something happens once, it's a fluke. If it happens twice, it is a coincidence. If it happens three times, it is a pattern. Breaking your pattern in even a simple way can improve things dramatically.

———•———

Although work can be a form of service, service is service, and work is work. When you do volunteer service, give as you feel moved to with no expectation of compensation. When you work, put your time and money together.

———•———

Learn to say "no" to things that result in taking on too much.

———•———

When you ask for help, what you get is often different than what you expect. Know what you need so that you know what to ask for.

———•———

State your need, and get on with life.

———•———

Do the research, and try not to jump on the first thing.

———•———

Think, decide, and act. Think about what is important for you and others, make a decision, and act on your own behalf.

———•———

Courage changes your life as much as wisdom.

———•———

There is more than one right way to do something.

———•———

Try to do more with less.

———•———

There IS enough.

———•———

An abundance mentality focuses on what IS and what CAN BE. A scarcity mentality focuses on what IS NOT. Let go of self-imposed deprivation, and move towards abundance thinking.

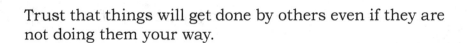

Trust that things will get done by others even if they are not doing them your way.

Work the solution, not the problem.

Know what and how much is really essential in your life.

The thing you need will always be right there when you need it.

It is okay to try something new. If it is not a success, it will not take you down.

No one is exempt from the rules.

An inability to manage emotions, such as loneliness or anger, can cause you to overspend or underspend your money.

———•———

Focus on thriving, not just surviving.

———•———

Clarity results from writing down expenses and talking about money issues.

———•———

If it is your bus, it will stop for you. If you missed the bus, it was not your bus.

———•———

Giving too much away to others is a form of self-sabotage.

———•———

Where the mind goes, the man will follow. You will manifest what is in your head and what you focus on.

———•———

What we receive is not just for us to have, it is about having it in order to give to others.

———•———

With time, energy, and money, do what creates balance in all areas of your life. Focus first on your needs, and then on your wants. Setting limits is a way of creating boundaries and balance. How are you spending your time? It is the only resource that cannot be replaced; manage it judiciously with appropriate limits.

———•———

You will have what you need when you need it.

———•———

If you are not ready to do something, wait.

———•———

The pain of letting go bears more fruit than the pain of trying to force your will in something that is not meant to be.

———•———

It is not necessary to shut down parts of yourself and just do one thing. Do many things in order to give life to the many different parts of yourself.

———•———

Learn what your limitations are and what you can and cannot do. You cannot be everything to everyone. Do what you can do, and do not do what you cannot do. You cannot do it all, and you should not even try.

———•———

Lead by example more than by words. Let people be attracted to you by doing the right thing.

Impatience can cause you to not fully appreciate getting what you want, because when you finally get it, you are already looking for the next thing.

If you find something to do with your hands, you will never be bored.

Make sure that you are honest in your communications with others and that you are really saying what you mean instead of just going along with other people's opinions.

It is not always necessary to answer people's questions right away.

Hold others responsible to do their own work, instead of taking it on yourself.

Some of the best results in your life can come from doing nothing.

Do the toughest thing that you dread the most first.

———•———

Create what you want in your life instead of waiting for somebody else to do it.

———•———

Compulsive spending is often fueled by jealousy, envy, and impulsivity. Ask yourself what you are really seeking. There will never be enough for you if you spend whatever you have until it is gone.

———•———

"Playing small" is choosing less than what you are in order to feel safe, not be intimidated, and to maintain an illusion of control.

———•———

People lose hope; situations do not. They turn around faster when you change your attitude.

———•———

Negotiate for what you want instead of just taking what people give you.

———•———

If you put principles and integrity first, everything else will work out.

Instead of trying harder, ask for help and do less.

Invest yourself more in what you are doing than in what other people are doing.

There is no perfect formula. Just because a tool works in one situation does not mean it will always be right in every situation. Guard against being too rigid by staying flexible and open to the possibilities of the present moment.

The more you give to others, the more you receive.

Yield in order to get what you want.

Forgiveness is an important part of attracting prosperity.

If you do your best, that is just fine.

———•———

Wait until the time is right to act.

———•———

When you feel a sense of inadequacy, acknowledge it and then clarify to see what is real and what is not. Then share it with someone and let it go.

———•———

Leave the past in the past, and start on a new road to constructive action.

———•———

Make the plan without planning the results.

———•———

Be willing to let go of old ideas.

———•———

Recognize your progress, acknowledge it, and use it to take the next step.

———•———

Deprivation and scarcity thinking can stem from a lack of nurturing, love, or support in your childhood.

———•———

Looking at one small aspect of a situation differently can change your whole perspective. It is not necessary to look at the whole thing differently to have a new perspective.

———•———

Use the gifts that you have today. If they are taken away, you will have had a full life.

———•———

Dishonesty is often motivated by fear of lack.

———•———

In work, know how to take care of yourself, and know when to stop.

———•———

The three main areas of life are work, home, and love. Experiencing change in any one of them can alter your sense of abundance.

———•———

Check your motives. If you want more emotional, spiritual, and financial prosperity, you will bring people into your life that will help you. If you want to be a victim, you will bring people into your life that will victimize you. If you want to be a complainer, you will bring people into your life to complain about. Examine your true intentions.

———•———

In some games, no one wins. If you are going to play games, make sure someone can win.

———•———

It is okay if you make a mistake. The world will not come apart. You will get another chance to do it right.

———•———

There is no need to fear or be intimidated by your clients. Take control by putting your real self out there.

———•———

It is not always necessary to plan what you are going to say in a particular situation, just let it come naturally and flow.

———•———

What do you really want? Sometimes, the curse of life is actually getting what you thought you wanted.

———•———

Buying things cannot make up for the lack of emotional care you experienced as a child. If you do not have the means to buy something, it is not supposed to be in your life.

———•———

There is enough money. Let go of the idea that there is not enough of anything in the world for you.

———•———

Under-spending is no better than overspending. Are you spending money for your wants or needs? Are they in balance? If not, try to spend more on your needs and less on your wants.

———•———

Urgency stems from fear, not from certainty.

———•———

The pursuit of prestige stems from the need for approval. It is rooted in pride and fear, rather than love. Just try to serve others and do a good job, without having to impress everybody.

———•———

One negative thing does not need to spoil other areas of your life that are good.

———•———

Living life abundantly means letting people in and not running away. When you want to run away, something inside of you may be coming up that you need to confront or deal with.

———•———

You are not a failure if you do not have all the answers today. In many instances, you will never have the answers.

———•———

If you do something wrong a number of times, you do not have to do it right the same number of times to break even.

———•———

Focus on your own responsibilities without getting distracted by interruptions or by what other people are doing.

———•———

Start working on things at your own level.

———•———

Show up and be honest, and whatever is meant to happen will happen.

———•———

You can change your life by changing your thoughts.

———•———

Decision- making does not always have to lead to action. A decision to delay a decision IS a decision. Deciding to do nothing IS a decision. Not making a decision IS making a decision.

———•———

Perfect is usually slightly more complicated than is actually realistic. Just do it. You do not need to do it perfectly. Try to make progress and move forward.

———•———

Become who you are rather than what you do.

———•———

What would you do if you had no fear or if time and money were not obstacles? This will tell you what is really in your heart and whether you are living in line with or against your values.

———•———

If you are stuck, take action. Trying to figure things out and overanalyzing are ways of avoiding action. It is impossible to figure it all out. It just is what it is. Trying to understand everything is a waste of your time.

———•———

When everyone does his share, no one gets burned out. It is not necessary to do it all yourself and feel the burden of doing more than your share. Just do your part.

———•———

Look at work as an opportunity to be of service to others and to fulfill your talents and potential. The higher up you are on the totem pole, the more people you are entrusted to serve.

———

The proper balance between unity and autonomy allows a person to flourish. Unity means allowing yourself to work with others in order to further your capacity and potential for growth. There are times when you must rely on other people. You cannot do everything by yourself. Autonomy involves giving yourself appropriate credit for your accomplishments and taking responsibility for your shortcomings. Autonomy also means that you do not always need to be validated by others. There are times when your power is within you.

———

Try to take thing at face value instead of reading too much into them and looking for hidden meanings. Most of what people do is not about you. They just do what they do. Be direct, clear, and assertive without sending or receiving coded messages. Say what you mean and mean what you say without being mean.

———

Sometimes you may use other people and their issues as excuses to keep your own life small and to avoid living your life fully. The possibilities in your life are restricted only by your own mind and imagination.

———

Remember that things get replenished. Much fear and worry are about the dwindling of resources.

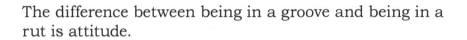

The difference between being in a groove and being in a rut is attitude.

Do the worst first.

In order to prosper, work with other people and delegate.

Your impression of how you think other people are doing does not need to be the measure of yourself.

Living fully is about having good things happen, not just about preventing bad things from happening.

No one can stifle your life except you.

Build a life of choice. This means letting go of things that do not work for you, and choosing what you like, including what you eat, wear, the people in your life, and who you want to be.

If something is beyond your power, then you did not fail when you did not make it happen.

Life is about more than staying safe.

If it is not a thought about an action or anything you can do, let it go.

Fearless means not letting fear stop you from doing something. It does not mean the absence of fear.

If you are not making mistakes, you are not reaching far enough.

Perfection is the compulsive need to modify, even if something is already well done.

You are usually the biggest thing standing in your way.

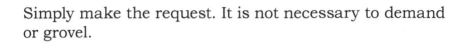

Simply make the request. It is not necessary to demand or grovel.

Recognize, reach out, accept, and act.

Participate in order to feel a sense of belonging.

Take the time to identify what you need, not just what you want.

Set your own agenda and goals.

Keep some time in your schedule free of commitments every week. This will allow room for new ideas and activities, as well as for self-restoration.

Focus on what can go right rather than on what can go wrong.

———◦———

When you trust someone to represent you, it is not necessary to micromanage them by imposing your fear-driven perfectionism on them. If it does not work out, remove them and make changes.

———◦———

It is your responsibility to discover what you want and take action in that direction. Even though you may not be in control of the results, you do have control over your footwork. If you move confidently in the direction of your dreams, you will have more success than you expect.

———◦———

There is a time to trust other people; you will not always have all the answers yourself.

———◦———

Codependency can lead to compulsively overscheduling, which limits prosperity.

———◦———

It is not possible to solve a problem by condemning it.

———◦———

It is okay to fail when things are impossible.

———◦———

If you build it, the people will come.

———•———

Try to participate in life rather than just being an observer. Get out from in front of the television and start living life instead of watching it.

———•———

Are you afraid to be inadequate, or are you afraid to excel?

———•———

Just because someone makes a request of you does not make them an authority. Recognize your own voice as your authority.

———•———

It is not necessary to pick up every challenge immediately. You can wait, develop a strategy to deal with it effectively, or not even deal with it at all.

———•———

Accept your limitations. Making commitments beyond what you know you can do reduces your prosperity.

———•———

What in your life has helped you to ask for help, and what in your life has kept you from asking for help?

———•———

What you have in your life today you truly deserve.

———•———

Procrastination leads to justification for missed opportunities. Try to keep your focus on what you are doing right now without letting yourself get distracted.

———•———

What really needs to be done? Stay away from doing things that do not need to be done just to stay busy. Sometimes the thing that needs to be done does not need to be done by you. Learn to delegate.

———•———

Figure out what you want to do and what you need to do.

———•———

It is never too late to reinvent yourself.

———•———

Overworking is quite costly.

———•———

Childhood emotional deprivation can lead to money issues, overspending, and stealing.

Show up for the life that you really want.

Allow the world to see you instead of remaining hidden in plain sight.

When you are at work, focus on your work, not the personalities and other distractions. Be mindful of your purpose for being there.

Like the seasons in nature, it is the natural order of things to have periods of action followed by periods of rest, followed by periods of action and then periods of rest.

The best advertisement is a good example.

The twenty-four hour rule: give yourself time to evaluate your truth before you act on something. In the midst of emotional confusion, wait twenty-four hours, think about it, ask for help, and then see where you are.

If you cannot recognize what already exists in your life, will you really appreciate receiving more?

———•———

Live life deliberately, and focus on what is important.

———•———

Low self-esteem will cause you to feel guilty about having more than others and want to give it away. Use what you have to help others, and let go of guilt about what you have.

———•———

It is okay for you to want what you want.

———•———

The way to grow to the next level is through practice, practice, practice, routine, and doing it over again.

———•———

Emotional insecurity leads to the fear of financial insecurity. Separate the emotions from the money, and deal with the situation and emotions for what they are. This entanglement becomes a challenge when your emotions have been controlled by someone through money.

———•———

What would you do if you were not afraid?

———•———

Strive to be fully self-supporting emotionally, physically, financially, and spiritually.

———•———

Overworking, overcommitting, and overbooking yourself will reduce emotional, physical, and spiritual prosperity.

———•———

The universe will provide you with everything you need, even money.

———•———

Self-sufficiency can be limiting. It is not necessary to be totally independent of others or totally dependent. Strive for interdependence and maintaining a balance between being self-sufficient and asking for help.

———•———

Pay more attention to what you have done than to what you have said.

———•———

Feeling deserving of success is essential to breaking the cycle of self-sabotage. To whom are you so loyal that you will not allow yourself to succeed?

You are enough, and there is enough for you.

At work, take responsibility when you are wrong, and deal with things as a professional.

Positive reinforcement and motivation foster prosperity more than trying to force compliance.

One way of dealing with ambiguity is to impose structure. Too little structure leads to nothing. Too much structure leads to rigidity. In rigidity, the rules become more important than the point of things.

The best leaders live by example, do not tell people what to do, and are not harsh.

When you need to say something, simply convey the information rather than being driven by fear of the other person's reaction.

Learn to delegate work instead of working yourself to death doing everything alone. It is okay if someone does a task differently than you do. They do not have to do things perfectly according to your standards. Avoid micromanaging other people; they have their own ways of doing things. Sometimes their way is better than yours. The way you do things is not necessarily the only way things can get done or the way it has to be.

Being "self-supporting" means that you pull your own weight. It does not mean that you are compulsively autonomous or that you cannot support others.

Take a regular inventory of what your efforts are producing. This includes an inventory of how your time is being spent.

When you are at work, focus on just doing your job. You only need to do your job.

If you want something you have never had, you may need to do something you have never done.

If you do not have something, it is possible that you are not supposed to have it.

———•———

Be grateful for what you have and also for what you do not have.

———•———

It is okay to feel grateful but still want more.

———•———

Budget more of your time by attending to your own business.

———•———

Strive to contribute rather than compete. Just be human beings together and maybe even allies.

———•———

No one can do it all. Ask for help. Taking things a piece at a time will help you not to feel overwhelmed. You cannot eat the elephant in one bite. Being fully self-supporting means asking for help when you need it.

———•———

Stealing can stem from resentment, a lack of faith, and a fear that you will not get enough.

———•———

If something does not work out, do something differently.

Right ambition is determined by motives.

You will achieve what you are working towards.

Ask for what you really want. You can have what you want if you are willing to ask for help and work for it.

An antidote to worry is to work hard.

You really do have everything that you need.

You do not have to solve the whole problem. You can just begin and then take small steps to work on the problem.

It is never too late to do anything as long as you are alive.

Prosperity is not about having stuff, money, and success. It comes through the spiritual power of love through servitude. Prosperity means having all that you need physically, emotionally, and spiritually to meet any circumstance, with enough left over to give wherever God might direct you. If nothing is ever enough, you do not have prosperity. If you do not appreciate what you already have, how could you possibly appreciate more? It is a state of mind.

7
SPIRITUAL GROWTH

God is either everything or nothing.

———•———

The benefits of having a relationship with God include understanding, sensitivity, peace, security, and stability.

———•———

Keep doing what you are doing until God tells you differently.

———•———

The things that come to you are meant to be yours. When you are not supposed to have something, God will take it away, and a new path will open up.

———•———

Find a way to invest your heart in the world. Visions are goals that can be material, concrete, emotional, or experiential. Your goals and visions are already inside of your heart and will manifest without too much strain. If you are living in alignment, they will not cause you to neglect doing the fundamentals. You can have a plan and take small steps to get there. Making them a reality is doing God's will.

———•———

If it is God's will for you to do something, He will increase your desire for it.

———•———

The order of the universe is God, self, others, things. Make sure that you have enough within yourself to be able to give to others.

———•———

Money is money. God is God. Money is not a substitute for God.

———•———

If God gives you the mission, He will also give you the strength.

———•———

Pray like God is in charge of everything, and work like you are in charge of everything.

———•———

Security does not come from how much money you have in the bank; it comes from your relationship with God.

———•———

There is always more than one person who can help you in any given situation. You do not need to expect everything from one person. When there is no one you can ask for help, it comes down to you and God. You can always ask God for help.

Grow up, be who you are, and use the gifts God has given you.

We love God by loving other people.

If there is something that you want or need, you will have it when God thinks you are ready for it. He gives you what you need when you need it. You may not get everything you want, but your needs will be met.

The tests can get harder as you move on in the spiritual journey. God will give you a constant workout so that you are spiritually fit. The testing of your faith will produce endurance and perseverance.

Gratitude builds faith.

Freedom is the release from illegitimate restriction.

The process of change is not always peaceful, but the end result of doing God's will is peace.

If you know how to worry, you know how to pray. When you pray, something always happens.

Seek God first, and all the other things you seek will be given to you.

If you try to solve an inside problem with an outside solution, the relief will only be temporary. An inside problem requires an inside solution, a spiritual solution.

Wisdom is gained through costly experience.

Spiritual people believe that the supernatural is natural.

God is real, and He rewards diligence.

Your primary job is to stay connected to God.

Whatever the problem is, the solution is spiritual.

You know you have experienced grace when you are in a different universe from where you had been stuck and you have no idea how you got there.

You have always been taken care of. It is not just luck.

Trust God; there are going to be people there to help you through.

The minute you accept something, it changes.

God will have His way in the end. Get on board.

Waiting is a big part of growth.

Death is not an ending; it is a transition.

It is not possible to worry and pray at the same time.

Goodness is always present, even when evil is there too.

Prayer is talking to God; meditation is listening to God.

When you are looking for God, it feels like God is finding you.

During the good times, give the credit to God. During the hard times, lean on God.

Life is lived forwards but understood backwards. Learn from your mistakes as well as from those of others.

Obey the unenforceable guidelines.

Grace will come in when you need it.

———•———

It is what you learn after you know it all that counts most.

———•———

What you need to deal with next will come up. You do not have to look for it.

———•———

You never know where life will take you. Life is to be enjoyed; let yourself be guided by the moment.

———•———

Let go of the fight for necessity. Grit and fierce determination do not necessarily result in anything.

———•———

When you need information, God will give it to you. All ideas come in their own time.

———•———

Step back and let life take its course. The more control you try to take, the more out of control life gets.

———•———

Religious people believe in hell. Spiritual people have been there.

There are two prayers: willingness and courage.

When you are gentle and easy with yourself, God can help you. It cannot happen when you are acting out of desperation.

You can bank on the grace of God no matter what you do or do not do.

Pray for something positive, instead of praying for something NOT to happen.

If you have ninety-nine percent doubt and one percent faith, try to live in that one percent.

Wait for answers instead of trying to force them.

There are unlimited possibilities, regardless of your age.

In order to develop a relationship with God, try to live in gratitude.

If you are supposed to know something, it will be revealed to you, and you will know it.

When you do not know what to do, turn to God and ask Him.

Any limits on God are the ones that you have placed.

It is not about losing your will to God's will. It is about aligning your will with God's will.

Slow down before changing direction.

Trust God instead of scamming your way through life and relying only on yourself.

God has supernatural power. Do not ask Him for crumbs while He is preparing a banquet for you.

The spiritual journey can restore your growth potential to that of a child. There is no limit to how far you can go.

It is not necessary to work so hard at making contact with God. All you have to do is be willing. You will be contacted.

Always be a beginner.

There is no moment when God is not there.

You may be powerless over something, but you are never helpless.

If God brings you to it, He will bring you through it.

God is in the details.

If you try too hard to find anything, you push it away.

It does not matter if you do not believe in God. He will come to you.

Whatever decision you make, it will be alright.

Take right action, and wait for grace to come in.

A spiritual awakening can be as simple as not doing the same thing again or doing it in a different way.

God's will is whatever is put in front of you that day.

Change happens; growth is optional. Choose wisely.

God removes the pressure from your life by giving you truth.

Adversity does not build character, it reveals it.

Turn your worries into prayers. Give them over to God; He is going to be up all night anyway.

A miracle is when preparation meets opportunity.

If you do not have a solution to a problem, the answer is acceptance.

What comes easily is God's will.

God's will is what you would do if you had all the facts.

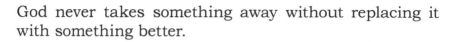

God never takes something away without replacing it with something better.

———•———

The way you learn what to do is by walking the path. What God wants from you, He puts right in front of you.

———•———

If you think about something all the time, it is going to manifest in your life.

———•———

Powerlessness means learning to yield when necessary.

———•———

Surrender is not submission; it is what happens when you stop fighting reality. Surrendering means letting something go. Surrender has many layers and levels and involves relaxing into the truth. The pain is not in the surrender. The pain is in the resistance to it.

———•———

The power of the truth lets you move on.

———•———

Life is about a series of lessons and constant learning.

———•———

When you are going through a tough time, something is coming out of you. God is detoxing or cleansing you of something that no longer serves you.

———•———

A spiritual connection can alleviate your negative response to life.

———•———

Do what is in front of you, and watch what God does.

———•———

Faith involves the patient belief that you will have what you need.

———•———

A spiritual awakening is a new state of consciousness and being.

———•———

What you resist, persists.

———•———

If you supply the willingness, God will provide you the strength.

Sometimes silence really is golden.

No choice is right or wrong; it is merely a different path.

Many times, the solution is to do nothing and pray.

Live in the spiritual world and visit the physical world instead of living in the physical world and visiting the spiritual world.

Attach to God, not your problems.

Try to consciously make contact with God in every hour of the day.

Let things come in their own time without being too demanding of God.

Stay connected to God first, and then let the other stuff come second.

———•———

Do you want to be profoundly changed, or do you just want your circumstances to be different?

———•———

Take a rest, and let God do the rest.

———•———

Keeping things simple means keeping only what is essential.

———•———

Whatever is going on in your life will ultimately work in your best interest.

———•———

There is a time for everything.

———•———

God shows up in your life in the little things.

———•———

If you are willing to go to any lengths to do the right thing, you usually will not need to.

Ask God to show you your right size in your body, work, and relationships – in everything.

A relationship with God results from focus and structure.

The solution has nothing to do with the problem.

Relax; you do not have to kill yourself trying to please God. Trying to please God is what pleases God.

Resentment and fear can block your relationship with God.

Until you shut the door on something, another one will not open.

Let go of needing excessive approval, validation, or availability from people. Get these things from God.

To have a relationship with God, all you have to do is seek Him.

People-pleasing is a form of making another person your God. People, places, things, and money cannot be your God. Remember who God is and who He is not.

Try not to spend your life just flipping the television channels and never watching a program. At some point you need to commit to something, pick a life, and live it.

Acceptance: "Oh God," "Oh well," "Okay."

Spirituality is putting God first.

There is good in everything that happens, even if you think it is bad. The growth cycle is pain, then change, then growth.

Belief that God exists is not the same as relying on God.

God will guide you to the right decision through prayer and meditation. You may not know the answer right now, but you will know it when the time comes. Grace comes at the moment you need it.

If you take reasonable actions, God will know that you are serious.

If you are feeling inner peace, it is God's will. If you are feeling inner turmoil, it is your will. Grace cannot come in if you are forcing your own will.

Your heart's desire is God's desire for you.

Faith is the belief that everything will be okay in the end. If things do not feel okay today, it is not the end.

A ship does not turn right around. First, it has to veer widely in the opposite direction. Then it turns.

Move towards things instead of away from them.

When things are free and easy, God's grace is working in your life.

When hope is gone, there is always grace.

Faith is hope with experience. It requires sacrifice and unselfish constructive action.

Letting go does not mean giving up, it means letting go of self-will.

Change happens in an instant. All the rest is preparation.

Make God, not money, your God. If you make money your God, there will never be enough.

A sincere belief in God can relieve you of worry and misery. Suffering is inevitable, but misery is optional.

God's will is for you to flow into your own truth instead of being a shrinking lamb.

When you align with God, you move and sway in life. If you become self-willed, you get trapped and stuck.

Keep your focus on your God rather than your problem.

Use the past to have faith in God. Things have worked out in the past, and they will work out again. The way is not always clear. You do not have to figure it all out. Trust that God will show you the way. You do not need to know all the answers.

It is not about asking God for what you want. It is about asking what God wants for you. How does He want to use you?

It is the opening up of yourself to a new thing that is spiritually healing rather than the perfection of doing it.

———•———

Get the boulders off the road. Let go of worry about the rocks and pebbles.

———•———

The only authority is God. If you get your way or do not get your way, it is because of God, not because of other people getting in the way.

———•———

Humility and an open mind can lead you to faith.

———•———

If you really want something, pray for God's will and God's timing.

———•———

When something remarkable happens, it is a wink from the universe.

———•———

No one can take God away from you.

———•———

No matter what is going on and how painful things are, it is going to be okay.

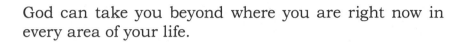

God can take you beyond where you are right now in every area of your life.

God can take you beyond where you are right now in
every area of your life.

How you do something is how you do everything.

Everything has a statute of limitations.

In the spiritual journey, nothing has changed, but everything is different.

Use the tool of evidence; when have you had this challenge before? Remember that God got you through it before. This will build your faith.

Power your life on more than just one (your own) battery.

You can have fear or faith, but you cannot have both at the same time.

In order to practice faith, make a decision, and let God work on it.

Pay attention to where things flow. This is God's will. When something is God's will, things fall into place. There is a "comfortable" factor with no battlefield. Where there is struggle, it is your own will.

Life is a roller coaster. Try to be in the car instead of strapped to the track.

Whether you remember it or not, God is with you every single moment.

Staying on the path of spiritual growth leads to increasing clarity and expansion of consciousness. Moving away from the path leads to vagueness and loss of consciousness.

If you do not ever feel discomfort, you are not growing. If you are not growing, you are dying.

Get as much information as possible in order to make a good decision. Talk to people, read, and educate yourself.

———•———

When you practice prayer and meditation, you find an inner strength within that you did not know you had. The longer you do it, the more the muscle builds.

———•———

Every thought is a form of prayer, regardless of the type of thought.

———•———

Spiritual growth precedes financial growth, and spiritual principles must come before material security. Money, property, and prestige do not really make you feel complete. Spirituality does.

———•———

God keeps us off balance so we can learn to lean on Him more.

———•———

Humility: stay green and grow. Get ripe and rot.

———•———

When you step up, God steps in.

Example is the best sermon.

There are no lightning bolts, only small nudges and inner voices.

The will of God will never take you where the grace of God will not protect you.

Everything can change in a day.

Not knowing is freedom.

God does not care about your disabilities; He cares about your availability.

Gently press the door. If it opens, it is God's will.

Self-examination is a path to freedom.

You can measure your spirituality by the quality of the connections with people in your life.

Difficulty, loss, and grief can either motivate you to act out in bad behavior or to try to get closer to God. The choice is yours.

When you keep showing up in life, God has infinite surprises for you.

Every addiction is an attempt to fill the hole in your soul with the wrong thing.

Greed is at the root of compulsion.

God's will is always mutually beneficial. Whatever is God's will is beneficial not only for you but also for those around you.

Living in faith or fear is a conscious choice.

Trade in your dependence on people for dependence on God. By strengthening your relationship with God, strength comes directly to you from God instead of filtered and watered-down through another person.

Be grateful that grace steps in before justice.

Life is not about being happy. It is about finding meaning.

There are big things happening in your life right now, but they will not be clear to you for about two or three more years.

It is important to look for the good in everything that happens. Things that seem terrible often open up a wonderful door in your life later on. You can only see this when you are past the doorway.

The quality of your life is determined by the focus of your attention.

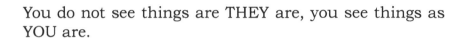

You do not see things are THEY are, you see things as YOU are.

Staying connected to God allows you more freedom and independence in life.

When you remain on the spiritual path, your worst times will become better than your best times used to be.

Wisdom comes from unlikely places.

If God brings you to it, then He will see you through it. The will of God will not take you where the care of God cannot keep you.

If you cannot live one day at a time, live one breath at a time.

Pray about the way you FEEL about things, not necessarily about the things themselves.

———•———

Each day has a gift for you. The art of living involves finding joy in something every single day. The beauty in your life is up to you.

———•———

A spiritual change means realizing that life does not have to be what it has always been.

———•———

"Today a peacock, tomorrow a feather duster." Try to not get too caught up in the external stuff.

———•———

If you are not shopping, what do the holidays mean to you?

———•———

Faith is hope with a track record.

———•———

Whatever the problem is, the answer is spiritual.

———•———

Life goes on after losses.

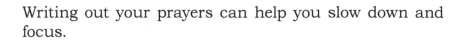

Writing out your prayers can help you slow down and focus.

Sometimes what God is trying to tell you takes a while to sink in.

Let life unfold slowly. God's timing is gradual and impeccable.

As long as you listen to your heart and to God, you will be more and more able to do what is right for you.

God will take away things that you do not need.

Change does not always happen when you see the light, it happens when you feel the heat.

Depend on and turn to God, not people, places, or things. They are not as important as you think they are.

———•———

Try to stay in the present moment and current day.

———•———

God manifests Himself in peace, joy, serenity, and integrity.

———•———

People need both sunshine and rain in order to grow.

———•———

Humility is a willingness to seek and follow God's will. It is a good barometer of your relationship with God.

———•———

Reserve judgment; you really do not know what is good and what is bad. Sometimes bad things turn out to be very good and vice versa.

———•———

The more you depend on God, the more magic there is in your life.

———•———

Let the visions for your life be spiritually-based.

———•———

Choose your thoughts wisely. Your life is an out-forming of your thoughts.

———•———

The more you struggle, the harder it gets. When you let go and relax, it turns out okay.

———•———

If you are rushing to make a decision, you are probably not listening to what God has to say.

———•———

Adversity can be a great teacher. Look for something positive to take from painful situations and experiences.

———•———

Most of the time, the worst outcome does not happen. Even when it does, there is always another side to the story.

———•———

It is never too late to try to work on anything.

———•———

Faith in God is more than believing in God. It is about trusting God to intervene in your life instead of being self-reliant.

When something leaves your life, there is a space that is open for a while. In the process of life, something else will come in later to fill that space.

You will find your treasure wherever you stumble and fall.

When you have spiritual maturity, God will change your character. If you are not yet spiritually mature, you can do your part by "acting as if." This means being generous when you feel greedy or being loving when you feel mean. Character traits have delicate little roots that go deep inside of you into different areas of life like the roots of a plant.

A change of character is evidenced by removal of the necessity to practice the old behavior, not necessarily the capacity to practice the old behavior. When your character has been transformed, you have a choice. Behaving differently will produce different results in your life and allow God to work on your behalf.

Wherever you are, you will not be there forever.

There is only so much you can do. Do what you can do, and let go of trying to do what is beyond your power. Relax and know that most things will be taken care of. Turn the rest over to God.

Spirituality is simplicity.

Everything that you have is fleeting. Appreciate what you have while you have it. Do not hang on to anything too tightly.

Life is a string of unanswered questions.

You will be given confidence and be led on your path through the practice of prayer and meditation. You will not have to figure it all out and force solutions.

God is a positive force in nature that causes things to more fully become themselves.

In order to use the power of God, all you need to do is invite Him in.

———•———

Trust your intuition; God really does have you covered.

———•———

Spiritual growth arises from experience rather than ideals.

———•———

Your eyes must be open to see things as they really are. To see things as better than they are, your eyes must be open to the fuller view.

———•———

God will make the changes that are necessary, not necessarily the changes you want.

———•———

There is no such thing as "too good to be true" in God's eyes.

———•———

Even when you cannot count on a particular person, you can count on God.

———•———

Spirituality is a path with heart.

———•———

If you looked back, would you be proud of the things you have done?

———•———

Spirituality is about relationship, not religion.

———•———

When the pain of not changing overcomes the pain of changing, you will change.

———•———

There is no difference between anyone.

———•———

Look to God for things you cannot count on from other people.

———•———

You have an unlimited source of strength and comfort available to you through God.

———•———

Sometimes your emotions can dominate you. However, spirituality can dominate emotions.

———•———

If you are feeling tense and frustrated, you are doing what you want to do. If you are feeling serene and peaceful, you are doing what God wants you to do. God's will comes to you through intuition, people, and opportunities.

———•———

God will come up with the solutions that you cannot find.

———•———

Whatever choice you make, you will be taken care of.

———•———

Be happy now because time passes.

———•———

God is your ultimate authority.

———•———

Life is what happens while you are making your plans.

———•———

If you go straight to prayer, you can bypass the worrying.

———•———

Reach for God before you make a decision.

———•———

Faith can be measured by how well you sleep at night.

———•———

Your life is already complete, whether or not you have what you think you need.

———•———

Keep your ears open. You never know where your answers will come from.

———•———

If you are going through hell, just keep going. Perfection is doing the best you can each day.

———•———

When you are heading the wrong way, God will try to wake you up with a feather. If you do not get it, he will wake you up with a brick.

———•———

Do one percent and let God do ninety-nine percent. Once you have done one hundred percent of your one percent, give it over to God.

Sanity is being reasonable.

At a certain point, you realize that you just want to enjoy your life and not get caught up in what does not matter.

Try to listen for what God tells you to do next instead of trying to force your own will.

Self-contentment comes from simplicity in your life.

There is always more to learn. Know what you do not know, and know that you do not need to know everything.

Everyone gets a turn to experience everything. This is the human condition.

Knowledge and power are what you get when you stop trying to give God directions and start listening for His will.

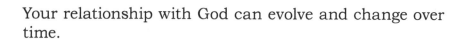

Your relationship with God can evolve and change over time.

There is no "there." Deciding you can be happy when you get "there" can be an endless trap. There is no one thing that will make you happy and content for good. Learn to be happy with who you are wherever you are.

You can either live in love or live in fear.

There is a good side to almost everything that happens. Practice looking for it.

Say what you want to say, do what you want to do, then get out of God's way.

God can help with just about anything. There is a spiritual solution to almost every problem.

Courage is gently acting with love in spite of fear.

God will honor your intentions when you are doing the best you can.

Focus on what a gift it is to be alive instead of wallowing in negativity.

Pray to see the love in your life.

Prayer is just a simple conversation with the one who loves you.

Prayer for others: "If there is a possibility of good, let X have it."

God is a gentleman. He will gently and quietly keep finding ways for you to see the truth.

Quiet the mind, open the heart.

There is always a way to move forward.

Awareness is the basis of spirituality.

Maturity is taking responsibility for yourself.

You are brought to the same lesson again and again until you get it. Each time the lesson comes it will be stronger in order to get your attention focused on the matter.

Patience is the key to paradise. Change takes a long time to happen. It can be massive yet slow. Continue to take action, and things will change in their own time. Accept God's timing.

Honesty is spiritual power and creates an authentic person.

In God's economy, nothing is wasted.

———•———

Once you fully accept a situation, God usually performs one of two miracles; either the situation changes, or the person changes.

———•———

Certainty about anything is a denial of God. There is not much we can really be certain about.

———•———

If you think your life will be ruined without the presence of another person, then you are making that person your God. Only God can be God. Everything else comes and goes.

———•———

There is always light on the other side of pain. Pain is inevitable, but suffering is optional. Suffering is what you do to yourself.

———•———

When you move away from being grounded in love, you end up out of power, which comes from God.

———•———

When you change the way you look at things, the things you are looking at change.

Having a spiritual life first can help you get something out of religion.

Spirituality is a change of perception.

God sometimes perform miracles in a physical or material way in order to help us cultivate faith and belief in Him.

Just do the best you can do in any situation.

Sometimes, a breakdown leads to a breakthrough.

You can see the stars when it gets dark enough. Be grateful for all that you have gone through. Growth comes out of adversity.

Who you are, including your talents and gifts, is God's gift to you. What you do with your life and your use of your talents are your gifts to God. You can show your love for God by giving back to others.

———•———

The more you align yourself with God, the more you can trust yourself and your decisions.

———•———

"How will you use this?"

———•———

Train yourself to let go of the things you fear losing the most.

———•———

Faith takes practice. Prayer and meditation are ways of putting faith into action.

———•———

Look forward more than you look back.

———•———

If it is for you to have, God will give it to you in His time. If you do not get something you want, God has something better in mind.

———•———

You are where you allow yourself to be.

Be the change you wish to see in the world.

Try to receive the agenda instead of dictating the agenda.

Everything that you turn over to God will turn to gold.

Blessings are given; happiness is a choice.

Patience is learned, not granted.

Try to keep your head and your heart aligned.

No matter what the circumstances, God is always working in your life and taking care of you. Nothing will ever change that.

Almost anything can become your teacher. Keep an open mind.

———•———

With God's help, you can change lifelong attitudes and patterns of behavior.

———•———

The antidote to fear is faith.

———•———

Writing, copying, and recopying can help you to study, learn, and grow. You can study spiritual principles the same way you would study a foreign language.

———•———

Prayer: talk to God, sit still, let go, be patient, and get the answer.

———•———

Serenity, courage, and wisdom are all gifts from God. You do not need to try to come up with these things by yourself.

———•———

Acceptance is not martyrdom. Courage is not control. Wisdom is not judgment.

———•———

You can accomplish unimaginable goals with spiritual help. Recommit yourself every day to furthering your spiritual growth.

———•———

Being surprised by grace is a gift to be cherished and remembered.

———•———

If you do not know what to do, do nothing. You will know when it is time to do something.

———•———

If you are having a problem with someone, it is really a problem with God.

———•———

Doing service work gives you a feeling of belonging.

———•———

If you rely on God, you will always be taken care of.

———•———

Do the next right thing, and have faith. Keep doing this, even if you do not know why you are doing what you are doing.

———•———

A stonecutter strikes a rock a thousand times before it cracks open. You may be making progress even when you do not think you are. Learn to accept the plateaus. Strive for perseverance and consistent small improvement.

———•———

Even if you are not sure whether there is a God, your life will be better if you act like there is a God.

———•———

You are not the source of love. You can reflect it or be an instrument of it, but God is the real source of love.

———•———

Grace is given moment by moment and is evidenced by God's acceptance of you exactly as you are. You will be given what you need in spite of yourself.

———•———

Life cannot be managed, it just happens.

———•———

If you are worried about what others are thinking of you, then you are probably judging others. If you stop judging others, then you will not feel judged. Try the spiritual challenge of spending one week without judging anyone or anything.

If it is spiritual, it is not urgent. If it is urgent, it is not spiritual.

Prayer: "God, thank you for what you have given me. Thank you for what you have taken away. Thank you for what is left."

No matter what, you will be okay.

Humility is accepting the truth and having compassion. It means recognizing your limits, taking your rightful place in the scheme of things, being teachable, and relying on God more than yourself. You are probably not as bad or as great as you think you are. Cultivate a "don't know" mind, and ask God for help with your life.

In order to get clarity, identify your intention.

Consistency is the key to a breakthrough. Do whatever it takes to grow to the next level.

Trust that the right thing will happen. There is no need to try so hard to work things out. God will work things out. All you need to do is show up, do your part, and trust.

It is hard to know where you are headed until you know where you are.

The power behind you is greater than the problem in front of you.

Try to see the world with soft eyes and compassion. Ask God to help you soften your responses to life.

God's gifts put man's best dreams to shame.

Faith requires action.

The journey is the destination. Walk boldly in the direction of your dreams.

Take action and God handles the reaction. God will do for you what you cannot do for yourself. But He will not do what you can do. If you do your part, He will do His.

———

You will be guided and cared for, no matter what happens in life.

———

You cannot worry your way to serenity. The answers will come to you when the time is right. Until then, keep on the right path, and do not try too hard to figure things out.

———

What can I do to see others as God sees them?

———

Let go of being addicted to outcomes.

———

God wants you to have joy and abundance.

———

When things happen easily, it is God's will. When things are very difficult, you may be trying to control something that is beyond your control.

———•———

All pain is God beckoning you to have a relationship with Him.

———•———

Whatever you did not get from your parents in childhood you can get in bits and pieces from other people now.

———•———

God helps those who ask.

———•———

You do not need to believe that God will help you, only that He could.

———•———

A journal is a "Godbox," a place where you send things to God to handle.

———•———

The more you focus on something, the bigger it gets.

———•———

Faith: you cannot know what you are going to do or say in a given situation until you arrive at that moment. Trust that the right ideas will come and the road will appear once you get there.

Sanity is the ability to make sound decisions.

If I did not do it and you did not do it, then the thing that restored you was God.

When you have a problem, wait, listen, learn, let yourself be guided, and do not worry about the outcome.

Some gifts are just given to you and other gifts you have to work for.

There is always something good that can come out of a conflict or a problem.

Focus on changing the things you can change instead of the things you should change.

Maintain a willingness to learn; you do not have to have a "way." Ask questions and be flexible.

Relationships are meant to change over time. Do not try to hang on to relationships forever. Cultivate new relationships on an ongoing basis.

To review your week, examine its high point and its low point.

There is always a choice; you can either focus on fear and what can go wrong, or you can focus on the grace in your life.

Ask for help. It is not necessary to go through anything alone.

Make a plan for serenity each day. Write down your worries in a journal, pray about them, and then let them go.

Rebellion against what you know is right is self-sabotage.

Worry does not change the outcome of a situation. God will take care of things.

———•———

Even if you crash or hit bottom, you can rebound and climb back up again.

———•———

Being consistent in thoughts, words, and actions reflects spirituality.

———•———

Life is about more than getting one chance and that is it. If you need to, do something over again.

———•———

All you have to do is receive the gifts in your life. You do not have to seek them.

———•———

Pain is often followed by a growth spurt.

———•———

See people as messages rather than as personalities.

———•———

If unexpected things happen, they were meant to be.

—•—

A spiritual awakening can be either slow or sudden and involves a profound change in perception and thinking. It is often the result of consistent effort. Finding your own voice and experiencing a personality change are fruits of a spiritual awakening.

—•—

Trust your intuition. This is often how God speaks to you.

—•—

Stumbling blocks are stepping stones.

—•—

It is not necessary to know who God is. It is necessary to know that you are not God.

—•—

Whatever you are going through will not last forever. It will pass.

—•—

Replace fear with faith.

—•—

Each day is an opportunity to change, improve, and create a better past.

Character liabilities are coping skills that have outlived their usefulness and no longer work.

Wisdom is a combination of intelligence and love.

If you face indecision while walking the spiritual path, follow the choice that feels right. It will usually work out for the best.

Be a spiritual warrior. Strive to see the essential goodness in yourself, others, and the world.